Moroccan

AND THE FOODS OF

North Africa

THE AUSTRALIAN
Women's Weekly

contents

This enticing selection of North African recipes is a scrumptious blend of familiar Moroccan, Algerian and Tunisian dishes with an equal number of modern takes on these cuisines whose origins are still based on traditional ingredients and cooking methods. I hope you enjoy this book as much as we did in compiling it, proving once and for all that there's much, much more to North African food than just couscous.

Pamela Clark

Food Director

North African food is a feast for the senses. No wonder it's becoming more and more popular – with its brilliant blend of spices and unusual combination of ingredients, not only does it taste and smell wonderfully exotic but, thanks to a liberal use of colourful components, it also looks especially enticing; it's difficult to imagine a cuisine with a more varied range of flavours.

With the Mediterranean lapping on its shores, North Africa shares culinary delights with its northern neighbours – heart-healthy olive oil and fresh vegetables are a staple, but where European Mediterranean countries rely on herbs for flavour, most North African dishes are based around aromatic spices, along with mint, parsley, harissa (a chilli paste, the use of which can be adjusted according to taste) and preserved lemon. In the souks, or markets, of the region, shoppers pick through vibrant stalls of cumin, coriander, saffron, ginger, cinnamon and paprika, mixing the spices at home into chermoulla, a blend used for marinating meat and fish. Luckily, we don't have to go so far for the ingredients, as they're all readily available on supermarket shelves.

Couscous, also available from supermarkets, is the North African equivalent of pasta, and a vital part of virtually every dinner, soaking up the flavour and juices from the main dish. When prepared with spices, vegetables, nuts and dried fruits, couscous is not only delicious, but is also healthy in its own right. Chickpeas and other pulses are also commonly used – rather than having to soak them overnight, it's worth keeping a few cans in your larder, as the tinned variety is just as good and far more convenient than the dried.

One characteristic feature of this region's food is the blend of sweet and savoury, and nowhere is this more in evidence than in the tagine, a rich stew named after the earthenware pot it's traditionally cooked in. You can use a normal casserole and still create an authentic dish where chicken may pair up with dates and honey, or lamb with apricots and citrus. The great thing you'll discover about North African food is that it can be as elegant or as down-to-earth as you like, but always with flavours that will transport you to an instantly sunny world.

NORTH AFRICAN FOOD

This recipe can be made 2 days ahead.

lamb and lima bean soup

preparation time 15 minutes (plus standing time) **cooking time** 2 hours 10 minutes **serves** 4

1 cup (200g) dried lima beans

2 tablespoons olive oil

3 frenched-trimmed lamb shanks (750g)

2 medium brown onions (300g), chopped coarsely

1 clove garlic, crushed

2 medium carrots (240g), chopped coarsely

2 trimmed celery stalks (200g),
chopped coarsely

2 cups (500ml) chicken stock

1 litre (4 cups) water

400g can chopped tomatoes

¼ cup coarsely chopped fresh dill

2 tablespoons lemon juice

1   Place beans in medium bowl, cover with water; stand overnight, drain.
2   Heat oil in large saucepan; cook lamb, in batches, until brown all over; remove from pan. Add onion, garlic, carrot and celery to same pan; cook, stirring, until softened.
3   Return lamb to pan with drained beans, stock and the water; bring to a boil. Simmer, covered, 1 hour, skimming surface occasionally.
4   Remove lamb shanks from pan. When cool enough to handle, remove meat from bones, discard bones; shred lamb. Return lamb to pan with undrained tomatoes; simmer, covered, 1 hour.
5   Just before serving, stir in dill and juice. Serve with toasted pitta bread, if desired.
per serving 7.5g fat; 849kJ (203 cal)

APPETISERS & SALADS

Beef mixture can be made the day before
and kept, covered, in the refrigerator.

beef and fig cigars

preparation time 30 minutes cooking time 30 minutes makes 48

20g butter

1 medium brown onion (150g), chopped finely

½ teaspoon ground cinnamon

2 cloves garlic, crushed

250g beef mince

¾ cup (150g) finely chopped dried figs

1 tablespoon finely chopped fresh chives

8 sheets fillo pastry

cooking-oil spray

½ cup (125ml) plum sauce

1 Melt butter in large frying pan; cook onion, cinnamon and garlic, stirring, until onion softens. Add beef; cook, stirring, until beef is browned. Stir in figs and chives; cool 10 minutes.

2 Meanwhile, preheat oven to 200°C/180°C fan-forced. Oil two oven trays.

3 Spray one pastry sheet with oil; cover with a second pastry sheet. Cut lengthways into three even strips, then crossways into four even strips.

4 Place 1 rounded teaspoon of the beef mixture along the bottom of one narrow edge of pastry strip, leaving 1cm border. Fold narrow edge over beef mixture then fold in long sides; roll to enclose filling. Place cigar, seam-side down, on tray; repeat process with remaining pastry and beef mixture.

5 Spray cigars lightly with oil. Bake, uncovered, about 10 minutes or until browned lightly. Serve with plum sauce.
   per cigar 0.9g fat; 146kJ (35 cal)

lamb and pine nut boats

preparation time 35 minutes cooking time 25 minutes makes 27

2 teaspoons olive oil

1 small brown onion (80g), chopped finely

2 cloves garlic, crushed

2 teaspoons ground cumin

400g lamb mince

1 medium tomato (150g), chopped finely

1 tablespoon finely chopped
fresh flat-leaf parsley

1 tablespoon lemon juice

2 tablespoons sumac

3 sheets ready-rolled shortcrust pastry

1 egg, beaten lightly

2 tablespoons pine nuts

1 tablespoon finely chopped
fresh flat-leaf parsley, extra

½ cup (140g) yogurt

1 Heat oil in small frying pan; cook onion, garlic and cumin, stirring, until onion softens. Place onion mixture in medium bowl with mince, tomato, parsley, juice and half the sumac; mix until combined.

2 Preheat oven to 200°C/180°C fan-forced. Oil two oven trays.

3 Cut each pastry sheet into nine squares. Brush two opposing sides of pastry square with beaten egg; place 1 level tablespoon of filling along centre of square. Bring egg-brushed sides together then push the two unbrushed sides inward to widen centre opening, making boat shape and showing filling. Sprinkle some of the nuts on exposed filling; place boat on tray. Repeat process, spacing boats 4cm apart on oven trays.

4 Bake, uncovered, about 20 minutes or until browned lightly and cooked through. Sprinkle with parsley.

5 Serve combined yogurt and remaining sumac in small bowl with boats.
per boat 8.4g fat; 581kJ (139 cal)

butter bean dip with pitta crisps

preparation time 8 minutes cooking time 8 minutes serves 8

This recipe can be made a day ahead.
Store pitta crisps in an airtight container.

1 clove garlic, crushed

¼ cup fresh flat-leaf parsley leaves

400g can butter beans, rinsed, drained

1 teaspoon ground cumin

⅓ cup (80ml) olive oil

6 pocket pitta, cut into sixths

1 Preheat oven to 200°C/180°C fan-forced.
2 Blend or process garlic, parsley, beans and cumin until combined. With motor operating, add the oil in a thin, steady stream until mixture is smooth.
3 Place pitta pieces on lightly oiled oven trays; bake about 8 minutes or until browned lightly.
4 Serve dip with pitta crisps.
   per tablespoon 5.5g fat; 493kJ (118 cal)

beetroot and orange salad

preparation time 10 minutes serves 8

3 x 400g jar mini baby beets, drained

1 cup fresh flat-leaf parsley, chopped coarsely

1 medium orange (240g), peeled, segmented

2 tablespoons red wine vinegar

2 tablespoons extra virgin olive oil

1 Combine beets, parsley and orange in medium bowl.
2 Combine vinegar and oil in screw-top jar; shake well.
3 Just before serving, add dressing to salad; toss gently.
   per serving 4.7g fat: 422kJ (101 cal)

Beetroot and dressing can be
prepared a day ahead.

beetroot, fennel and lentil salad

preparation time 30 minutes cooking time 1 hour serves 6

3 medium beetroot (1.5kg), trimmed

1 tablespoon olive oil

1 medium fennel bulb (300g)

400g can brown lentils, rinsed, drained

100g wild rocket leaves

200g fetta cheese, sliced thinly

DRESSING

½ cup (125ml) olive oil

2 tablespoons lemon juice

½ teaspoon white sugar

2 teaspoons finely chopped fresh fennel fronds

1 Preheat oven to 180°C/160°C fan-forced.

2 Combine beetroot in small baking dish with oil. Bake about 1 hour or until tender. When cool, peel beetroot then chop coarsely.

3 Finely chop enough of the fennel fronds to give the 2 teaspoons needed for the dressing. Slice fennel bulb thinly.

4 Combine dressing ingredients in screw-top jar; shake well.

5 Toss fennel, lentils and rocket in large bowl with half the dressing. Add beetroot; toss gently. Top with fetta; drizzle with remaining dressing.
   per serving 10.3g fat; 945kJ (226 cal)

Recipe can be prepared a day ahead. Add the dressing up to three hours before serving.

Moroccan seasoning is available from most Middle-Eastern food stores, spice shops and major supermarkets.

tomato, olive and radish salad

preparation time 15 minutes (plus refrigeration time) **serves** 8

1½ cups (180g) seeded black olives

200g grape tomatoes

14 medium red radishes (490g), trimmed, quartered

200g button mushrooms, halved

½ cup fresh flat-leaf parsley leaves

DRESSING

2 teaspoons moroccan seasoning

½ teaspoon ground coriander

½ teaspoon sweet paprika

2 tablespoons red wine vinegar

⅓ cup (80ml) extra virgin olive oil

1   Combine dressing ingredients in screw-top jar; shake well.
2   Combine salad ingredients in medium bowl with the dressing. Cover; refrigerate at least two hours before serving.
per serving 9.5g fat; 506kJ (121 cal)

chermoulla chicken and chickpea salad

preparation time 25 minutes (plus standing time) cooking time 20 minutes serves 4

1 cup (200g) dried chickpeas

4 single chicken breast fillets (800g)

1 medium red capsicum (200g), chopped finely

1 medium green capsicum (200g), chopped finely

2 large egg tomatoes (180g), chopped finely

1 small brown onion (80g), chopped finely

2 tablespoons lemon juice

CHERMOULLA

½ cup finely chopped fresh coriander

½ cup finely chopped fresh flat-leaf parsley

3 cloves garlic, crushed

2 tablespoons white wine vinegar

2 tablespoons lemon juice

1 teaspoon sweet paprika

½ teaspoon ground cumin

2 tablespoons olive oil

1   Place chickpeas in large bowl, cover with cold water; stand overnight, drain. Rinse under cold water; drain. Cook chickpeas in medium saucepan of boiling water, uncovered, until just tender; drain. Rinse under cold water; drain.

2   Meanwhile, combine ingredients for chermoulla in large bowl; reserve half the chermoulla for chickpea salad.

3   Place chicken in bowl with remaining chermoulla; turn to coat chicken. Cook chicken, in batches, on heated oiled grill plate (or grill or barbecue) until cooked through. Cover to keep warm.

4   Place chickpeas in large bowl with capsicums, tomato, onion and reserved chermoulla; toss gently to combine. Serve chickpea salad with sliced chicken; drizzle with juice.

per serving 21.6g fat; 1994kJ (477 cal)

Orange flower water is often used in Moroccan cooking for its cooling effect. In this salad, a teaspoon of fragrant orange flower water is used to sweeten the sharp taste of the radish. You can buy bottles of orange flower water at selected supermarkets, delicatessens and Middle-Eastern food stores.

orange and radish salad

preparation time 30 minutes serves 4

6 large seedless oranges (1.8kg)

4 large red radishes (200g), sliced thinly

½ small red onion (50g), sliced finely

1 cup (180g) niçoise olives, seeded

LEMON DRESSING

1 clove garlic, crushed

½ teaspoon sweet paprika

½ teaspoon ground cumin

2 tablespoons lemon juice

2 tablespoons olive oil

¼ teaspoon white sugar

2 tablespoons finely chopped fresh parsley

1 teaspoon orange flower water

½ teaspoon ground cinnamon

1 Combine ingredients for lemon dressing in screw-top jar; shake well.
2 Peel oranges, removing white pith; slice thinly.
3 Overlap alternate slices of orange and radish around edge of serving plate; overlap remaining slices in centre. Top with onion and olives; drizzle with dressing.
per serving 11.4g fat; 1020kJ (244 cal)

You need to purchase a large barbecued chicken weighing approximately 900g for this recipe.

moroccan couscous and chicken salad

preparation time 10 minutes cooking time 5 minutes serves 4

1 cup (250ml) vegetable stock

1½ cups (300g) couscous

1 medium red onion (170g), sliced thinly

3 cups (480g) shredded barbecued chicken

½ cup (75g) coarsely chopped dried apricots

½ cup (80g) sultanas

¼ cup finely chopped fresh mint

1 tablespoon pine nuts

2 teaspoons cumin seeds

¾ cup (180ml) french dressing

1 Bring stock to a boil in large saucepan; remove from heat. Stir in couscous. Cover; stand about 5 minutes or until stock is absorbed, fluffing with fork occasionally. Stir in onion, chicken, apricot, sultanas and mint.

2 Meanwhile, dry-fry nuts and seeds in small frying pan over low heat until just fragrant. Add to couscous with dressing; toss gently to combine.
per serving 10.5g fat; 2625kJ (628 cal)

After sundown during Ramadan, many Muslims in Morocco and other North African countries break the day's fast by starting their meal with this hearty soup. Recipes vary from family to family, but chickpeas and lamb always feature.

harira

preparation time 25 minutes (plus standing time) cooking time 2 hours 15 minutes serves 8

1 cup (200g) dried chickpeas

20g butter

2 medium brown onions (300g), chopped finely

2 trimmed celery stalks (200g), chopped finely

2 cloves garlic, crushed

4cm piece fresh ginger (20g), grated

1 teaspoon ground cinnamon

½ teaspoon ground black pepper

pinch saffron threads

500g diced lamb

3 large tomatoes (660g), seeded, chopped coarsely

2 litres (8 cups) hot water

½ cup (100g) brown lentils

2 tablespoons plain flour

½ cup (100g) white long-grain rice

½ cup firmly packed fresh coriander leaves

2 tablespoons lemon juice

1   Place chickpeas in large bowl, cover with water; stand overnight, drain. Rinse under cold water; drain.

2   Heat butter in large saucepan; cook onion, celery and garlic, stirring, until onion softens. Add ginger, cinnamon, pepper and saffron; cook, stirring, about 2 minutes or until fragrant. Add lamb; cook, stirring, about 5 minutes or until lamb is browned.

3   Add chickpeas and tomato; cook, stirring, about 5 minutes or until tomato softens.

4   Stir in the water; bring to a boil. Simmer, covered, 45 minutes. Add lentils; simmer, covered, 1 hour.

5   Blend flour with ½ cup of the slightly cooled cooking liquid in small bowl; stir into lamb mixture with rice. Cook, stirring, until mixture boils and thickens. Stir coriander and juice into harira just before serving.
per serving 13.4g fat; 1364kJ (326 cal)

algerian chicken and chickpea soup

preparation time 20 minutes cooking time 50 minutes serves 6

2 tablespoons olive oil

350g chicken breast fillets

1 large brown onion (200g), chopped finely

2 cloves garlic, crushed

4cm piece fresh ginger (20g), grated

1½ teaspoons ground cumin

1½ teaspoons ground coriander

1 teaspoon ground turmeric

½ teaspoon sweet paprika

1 cinnamon stick

¼ cup (35g) plain flour

1 litre (4 cups) chicken stock

1 litre (4 cups) water

2 x 300g cans chickpeas, rinsed, drained

2 x 400g cans crushed tomatoes

2 tablespoons finely chopped preserved lemon

1 tablespoon coarsely chopped fresh coriander

1 Heat half the oil in large frying pan; cook chicken, uncovered, about 10 minutes or until browned both sides and cooked through. Cool; shred chicken coarsely.

2 Heat remaining oil in large saucepan; cook onion, garlic and ginger, stirring, until onion softens. Add spices; cook, stirring, until fragrant.

3 Add flour; cook, stirring, until mixture bubbles and thickens. Gradually stir in stock and the water; cook, stirring, until mixture comes to a boil. Simmer, uncovered, 20 minutes.

4 Add chickpeas and undrained tomatoes, bring to a boil; simmer, uncovered, 10 minutes.

5 Add chicken and lemon; stir soup over heat until hot. Just before serving, stir in fresh coriander.
   per serving 11.3g fat; 1205kJ (288 cal)

warm chicken tabbouleh

preparation time 15 minutes (plus standing time) cooking time 15 minutes serves 4

1 cup (160g) burghul

500g chicken tenderloins, sliced thinly

2 cloves garlic, crushed

¾ cup (180ml) lemon juice

¼ cup (60ml) olive oil

250g cherry tomatoes, halved

4 green onions, chopped coarsely

1 cup coarsely chopped fresh flat-leaf parsley

1 cup coarsely chopped fresh mint

1 Place burghul in small bowl, cover with boiling water; stand 15 minutes, drain. Squeeze out as much excess water as possible.

2 Meanwhile, combine chicken, garlic, a quarter of the juice and 1 tablespoon of the oil in medium bowl; stand 5 minutes. Drain; discard marinade.

3 Heat 1 tablespoon of the oil in wok; stir-fry chicken mixture, in batches, until chicken is browned and cooked through. Cover to keep warm.

4 Place burghul, tomato and onion in wok. Stir-fry until onion softens. Remove from heat; add chicken mixture, parsley, mint, remaining juice and remaining oil, toss gently to combine.

per serving 21.6g fat; 1843kJ (441 cal)

This colourful salad from the Tunisian capital of Tunis, tastes as good as it looks. North Africans like their food highly spiced and, while this recipe only includes two chillies, you can increase or decrease the quantity as you like.

You can omit the canned tuna and serve the salad with fresh char-grilled tuna, if you prefer.

tunisian tuna salad

preparation time 30 minutes cooking time 3 minutes serves 4

2 hard-boiled eggs, chopped finely

1 medium green capsicum (200g), chopped finely

2 medium tomatoes (300g), seeded, chopped finely

4 green onions, chopped finely

2 drained anchovy fillets, chopped finely

¼ cup (30g) seeded green olives, chopped finely

2 fresh small red chillies, chopped finely

2 teaspoons finely chopped fresh mint leaves

185g can tuna, drained, flaked

1 tablespoon drained baby capers, rinsed

HARISSA-STYLE DRESSING

2 tablespoons olive oil

1 clove garlic, crushed

1 teaspoon coriander seeds

1 teaspoon caraway seeds

1 tablespoon lemon juice

2 tablespoons red wine vinegar

1   Make harissa-style dressing.
2   Combine salad ingredients in medium bowl; drizzle over dressing, toss gently. Serve with flat bread, if desired.
    HARISSA-STYLE DRESSING Heat oil in small pan, add garlic and seeds; cook, stirring, until fragrant. Stir in juice and vinegar.
    per serving 14.3g fat; 886kJ (212 cal)

roasted eggplant with spiced rice

preparation time 10 minutes cooking time 30 minutes serves 4

3 medium eggplants (900g)

⅓ cup (80ml) extra virgin olive oil

2 cloves garlic, sliced thinly

1 tablespoon extra virgin olive oil, extra

1 tablespoon finely chopped
fresh flat-leaf parsley

1 tablespoon finely chopped fresh mint

SPICED RICE

30g butter

1 medium brown onion (150g), chopped finely

1 clove garlic, crushed

3 cardamom pods, bruised

½ cinnamon stick

2 cups (400g) basmati rice

1 cup (250ml) vegetable stock

1 cup (250ml) water

¼ cup (40g) roasted pine nuts

1 Preheat oven to 220°C/200°C fan-forced.

2 Cut eggplants into 3cm slices crossways; discard ends. Heat one-third of the oil in large frying pan; cook one-third of the eggplant until browned on both sides. Transfer to large shallow baking dish. Repeat with remaining oil and eggplant slices.

3 Sprinkle eggplant with garlic; bake, in oven, about 20 minutes or until eggplant is tender.

4 Meanwhile, make spiced rice.

5 Drizzle eggplant with extra oil; top with parsley and mint. Serve with spiced rice.

SPICED RICE Melt butter in medium saucepan. Add onion, garlic, cardamom and cinnamon; cook, stirring, without browning, until onion is softened. Add rice; stir to coat in butter mixture. Stir in stock and the water; bring to a boil then simmer, covered, about 15 minutes or until stock is absorbed. Remove from heat; stand, covered, 5 minutes. Stir in nuts.
per serving 33.1g fat; 2997kJ (717 cal)

VEGETABLE DISHES

orange and honey glazed carrots

preparation time 10 minutes **cooking time** 20 minutes **serves** 8

This recipe can be made several hours ahead; reheat just before serving.

30g butter

1 tablespoon olive oil

6 medium carrots (720g), sliced thickly

2 tablespoons white sugar

1 tablespoon finely chopped fresh flat-leaf parsley

1 tablespoon balsamic vinegar

1 Heat butter and oil in large frying pan, add carrots; cook, covered, until just tender.

2 Add sugar; cook, stirring, about 10 minutes or until carrots caramelise. Stir in parsley and vinegar.

per serving 5.4g fat; 376kJ (90 cal)

fried spiced potatoes

preparation time 5 minutes **cooking time** 25 minutes **serves** 4

1kg baby new potatoes

2 tablespoons olive oil

1 tablespoon black mustard seeds

1 teaspoon freshly ground black pepper

1 tablespoon coarsely chopped fresh flat-leaf parsley

1 Boil, steam or microwave potatoes until just tender; drain.

2 Heat oil in large frying pan; cook potatoes, stirring, until browned lightly.

3 Add mustard seeds; cook, stirring, about 1 minute or until seeds pop.

4 Add remaining ingredients; toss gently.

per serving 9.5g fat; 1033kJ (247 cal)

grilled eggplant with tabbouleh

preparation time 15 minutes (plus refrigeration time) cooking time 10 minutes serves 4

3 small tomatoes (270g)

¼ cup (40g) burghul

2 large eggplants (1kg)

⅓ cup (80ml) extra virgin olive oil

4 cups coarsely chopped fresh flat-leaf parsley

1 cup coarsely chopped fresh mint

1 medium red onion (170g), chopped finely

2 tablespoons lemon juice

1 Chop tomatoes finely, retaining as much juice as possible. Place tomato and juice on top of the burghul in small bowl; cover, refrigerate 2 hours or until burghul is soft.

2 Cut each eggplant into 8 wedges. Brush eggplant with half the oil; cook on heated grill plate (or grill or barbecue) about 10 minutes or until browned and tender.

3 Meanwhile, combine tomato mixture with the parsley, mint, onion, juice and remaining oil.

4 Serve tabbouleh with eggplant.
per serving 19.5g fat; 1225kJ (293 cal)

roasted vegetables with eggplant puree

preparation time 20 minutes cooking time 50 minutes serves 4

1 large green capsicum (350g)

2 large red capsicums (700g)

2 large yellow capsicums (700g)

2 medium eggplants (600g)

2 cloves garlic, unpeeled

¼ cup (60ml) lemon juice

2 teaspoons tahini

400g okra, trimmed

cooking-oil spray

350g mushrooms, sliced thickly

250g cherry tomatoes

12 yellow patty-pan squash (360g), halved

¾ cup loosely packed fresh basil leaves

1 teaspoon sumac

1 Preheat oven to 220°C/200°C fan-forced. Lightly oil 2 baking dishes.

2 Quarter capsicums; discard seeds and membranes; place, skin-side up, in baking dishes. Using fork prick eggplants all over; place in baking dish with garlic. Roast vegetables, uncovered, about 30 minutes or until skins blister. Cover capsicum pieces with plastic or paper for 5 minutes; peel away skin then slice capsicum thickly. Cover to keep warm.

3 When cool enough to handle, peel eggplants and garlic. Coarsely chop eggplants; finely chop garlic. Combine eggplant and garlic in medium bowl with juice and tahini; cover to keep warm.

4 Place okra onto oiled oven tray; spray with oil. Roast, uncovered, about 20 minutes or until just tender.

5 Meanwhile, cook mushrooms in large lightly oiled frying pan, stirring, until tender. Add tomatoes and squash; cook, covered, until tomatoes just soften.

6 Combine capsicum, tomato mixture and okra in large bowl with basil; divide among serving plates, top with eggplant mixture. Sprinkle with sumac; serve immediately.
per serving 3.1g fat; 759kJ (181 cal)

The crumb mixture can be made several hours ahead; cook zucchini just before serving.

If zucchini flowers are not available, substitute small zucchini quartered lengthways.

fried zucchini with pine nuts and currants

preparation time 15 minutes cooking time 15 minutes serves 8

¼ cup (60ml) extra virgin olive oil

40g butter

2 thick slices ciabatta, crusts removed, chopped finely into cubes

2 cloves garlic, crushed

1 tablespoon roasted pine nuts, chopped coarsely

1 teaspoon finely grated lemon rind

2 tablespoons finely chopped fresh flat-leaf parsley

1 tablespoon dried currants

24 tiny zucchini with flowers attached

1 Heat half the oil and half the butter in large frying pan, add bread cubes; cook, stirring, until browned lightly. Add garlic; cook, stirring, until fragrant. Stir in nuts, rind, parsley and currants. Transfer to medium bowl; cover to keep warm.

2 Heat remaining oil and butter in same pan, add zucchini; cook, covered, until browned lightly and just tender.

3 Serve zucchini sprinkled with bread mixture.
   per serving 12.6g fat; 610kJ (146 cal)

Tamarind is the product of a native tropical African tree that grows as high as 25 metres. The tree produces clusters of brown "hairy" pods, each of which is filled with seeds and a viscous pulp that are dried and pressed into the blocks of tamarind found in supermarkets and Asian food stores.

potato and cheese kofta with tomato tamarind sauce

preparation time 30 minutes cooking time 35 minutes (plus standing time) serves 4

2 medium potatoes (400g)

2 tablespoons finely chopped fresh coriander

½ cup (75g) roasted unsalted cashews, chopped finely

½ cup (60g) frozen peas, thawed

vegetable oil, for deep-frying

4 hard-boiled eggs, halved

CHEESE

1 litre (4 cups) milk

2 tablespoons lemon juice

TOMATO TAMARIND SAUCE

1 tablespoon olive oil

1 clove garlic, crushed

3cm piece fresh ginger (15g), grated

½ teaspoon dried chilli flakes

1 teaspoon ground cumin

1 teaspoon ground coriander

½ teaspoon mustard seeds

¼ cup (85g) tamarind concentrate

2 x 400g cans crushed tomatoes

1   Make cheese. Make tomato tamarind sauce.

2   Meanwhile, boil, steam or microwave potato until tender; drain.

3   Mash potato in large bowl; stir in cheese, coriander, nuts and peas.

4   Heat oil in wok; deep-fry level tablespoons of the potato (kofta) mixture, in batches, until cooked through. Drain on absorbent paper.

5   Add koftas to tomato tamarind sauce; simmer, uncovered, 5 minutes. Divide koftas and sauce among serving plates; top with egg.

CHEESE Bring milk to a boil in medium saucepan; remove from heat, stir in juice. Cool 10 minutes. Pour through muslin-lined sieve into medium bowl; stand cheese mixture in sieve over bowl 40 minutes. Discard liquid in bowl.

TOMATO TAMARIND SAUCE Heat oil in large saucepan; cook garlic and ginger, stirring, until fragrant. Add chilli, spices and seeds; cook, stirring, 1 minute. Add tamarind and undrained tomatoes; bring to a boil. Simmer, uncovered, 5 minutes.

per serving 29.7g fat; 144kJ (513 cal)

spicy roasted pumpkin couscous

preparation time 10 minutes cooking time 20 minutes serves 4

1 tablespoon olive oil

2 cloves garlic, crushed

1 large red onion (300g), sliced thickly

500g pumpkin, peeled, chopped coarsely

3 teaspoons ground cumin

2 teaspoons ground coriander

1 cup (200g) couscous

1 cup (250ml) boiling water

20g butter

2 tablespoons coarsely chopped
fresh flat-leaf parsley

1 Preheat oven to 220°C/200°C fan-forced.

2 Heat oil in medium flameproof baking dish; cook garlic, onion and
pumpkin, stirring, until vegetables are browned lightly. Add spices;
cook, stirring, about 2 minutes or until fragrant.

3 Roast pumpkin mixture, uncovered, in oven, about 15 minutes or until
pumpkin is just tender.

4 Meanwhile, combine couscous with the water and butter in large heatproof
bowl; cover, stand about 5 minutes or until liquid is absorbed, fluffing with
fork occasionally.

5 Add pumpkin mixture to couscous; stir in parsley.
per serving 9.8g fat; 1361kJ (325 cal)

spinach with burghul and chickpeas

preparation time 20 minutes cooking time 10 minutes serves 4

1 large red capsicum (350g)

1 cup (160g) burghul

1 cup (250ml) boiling water

420g can chickpeas, rinsed, drained

1 trimmed celery stalk (100g), chopped finely

50g baby spinach leaves

SUMAC AND HERB DRESSING

1 tablespoon sesame seeds

2 tablespoons sumac

1 tablespoon fresh thyme leaves

1 tablespoon coarsely chopped fresh oregano

½ cup (125ml) lime juice

1 tablespoon olive oil

1 clove garlic, crushed

1 Quarter capsicum; discard seeds and membranes. Roast under grill or in very hot oven, skin-side up, until skin blisters and blackens. Cover capsicum pieces with plastic or paper for 5 minutes; peel away skin then slice capsicum thinly.

2 Meanwhile, place burghul in medium bowl, cover with the boiling water; stand about 10 minutes or until burghul softens and water is absorbed.

3 Combine ingredients for sumac and herb dressing in small bowl.

4 Place burghul and capsicum in large bowl with chickpeas, celery, spinach and dressing; toss gently.
   per serving 8.6g fat; 1150kJ (275 cal)

pumpkin and split pea tagine

1 cup (200g) green split peas

1 tablespoon olive oil

1 medium brown onion (150g), chopped finely

2 cloves garlic, crushed

2 teaspoons ground coriander

2 teaspoons ground cumin

2 teaspoons ground ginger

1 teaspoon sweet paprika

1 teaspoon ground allspice

1kg pumpkin, diced into 3cm pieces

425g can crushed tomatoes

1 cup (250ml) water

1 cup (250ml) vegetable stock

2 tablespoons honey

200g green beans, trimmed, chopped coarsely

¼ cup coarsely chopped fresh coriander

1 Cook split peas in medium saucepan of boiling water, uncovered, until just tender; drain. Rinse under cold water; drain.

2 Meanwhile, heat oil in large saucepan; cook onion, stirring, until softened. Add garlic and spices; cook, stirring, about 2 minutes or until fragrant. Add pumpkin; stir pumpkin to coat in spice mixture.

3 Stir in undrained tomatoes, the water and stock; bring to a boil. Simmer, uncovered, about 20 minutes or until pumpkin is just tender. Stir in honey then beans and peas; simmer, uncovered, about 10 minutes or until beans are just tender. Remove from heat; stir in coriander. Serve with steamed couscous, if desired.

per serving 7g fat; 1484kJ (355 cal)

Chermoulla is a Moroccan blend of herbs and spices traditionally used for preserving or seasoning meat and fish. We use our chermoulla blend here as a quick baste for chicken, but you also can make it for use as a sauce or marinade.

chicken chermoulla

preparation time 10 minutes cooking time 20 minutes serves 4

700g chicken thigh fillets, sliced thinly

½ cup coarsely chopped
fresh flat-leaf parsley

1 tablespoon finely grated lemon rind

1 tablespoon lemon juice

2 teaspoons ground turmeric

1 teaspoon cayenne pepper

1 tablespoon ground coriander

1 medium red onion (170g), chopped finely

2 tablespoons olive oil

1 cup (200g) red lentils

2½ cups (625ml) chicken stock

200g baby spinach leaves

½ cup coarsely chopped fresh coriander

½ cup coarsely chopped fresh mint

1 tablespoon red wine vinegar

⅓ cup (95g) yogurt

1 Combine chicken, parsley, rind, juice, spices, onion and half the oil in large bowl. Heat large frying pan; stir-fry chicken mixture, in batches, until chicken is browned and cooked through.

2 Meanwhile, combine lentils and stock in large saucepan. Bring to a boil; simmer, uncovered, about 8 minutes or until just tender; drain. Place lentils in large bowl with spinach, coriander, mint and combined vinegar and remaining oil; toss gently.

3 Serve chicken on lentil mixture; drizzle with yogurt.
per serving 24.9g fat; 2191kJ (524 cal)

MEAT, POULTY & FISH

coriander and chilli grilled chicken fillets

preparation time 10 minutes cooking time 15 minutes serves 4

6 chicken thigh fillets (660g), halved

CORIANDER CHILLI SAUCE

8 green onions, chopped coarsely

3 cloves garlic, quartered

3 fresh small red chillies, chopped coarsely

¼ cup loosely packed fresh coriander leaves

1 teaspoon white sugar

1 tablespoon fish sauce

¼ cup (60ml) lime juice

CHICKPEA SALAD

2 x 300g cans chickpeas, rinsed, drained

2 medium egg tomatoes (150g), chopped coarsely

2 green onions, chopped finely

2 tablespoons lime juice

1 cup coarsely chopped fresh coriander

1 tablespoon olive oil

1 Make coriander chilli sauce.
2 Cook chicken, in batches, on heated oiled grill plate (or grill or barbecue) until almost cooked through. Brush about two-thirds of the coriander chilli sauce all over chicken; cook further 5 minutes or until chicken is cooked through.
3 Meanwhile, combine ingredients for chickpea salad in large bowl; toss gently.
4 Serve chickpea salad with chicken; sprinkle with remaining coriander chilli sauce.
   CORIANDER CHILLI SAUCE Blend or process onion, garlic, chilli, coriander and sugar until finely chopped. Add sauce and juice; blend until well combined.
   per serving 18.8g fat; 1659kJ (397 cal)

chicken with almonds and date sauce

preparation time 10 minutes cooking time 15 minutes serves 4

1 tablespoon olive oil

1 large brown onion (200g), sliced thinly

1½ teaspoons ground cinnamon

2 teaspoons finely grated orange rind

¼ teaspoon cayenne pepper

1½ cups (375ml) chicken stock

½ cup (70g) seeded dates, chopped coarsely

1 large barbecued chicken (900g), quartered

1 cup (250ml) orange juice

1 cup (250ml) water

2 cups (400g) couscous

20g butter

¼ cup (35g) roasted slivered almonds

1 Heat oil in large frying pan; cook onion, stirring, until browned lightly. Add cinnamon, rind, cayenne and stock; bring to a boil. Simmer, uncovered, 4 minutes. Add dates and chicken; stir until mixture is heated through.

2 Meanwhile, combine juice and the water in large saucepan; bring to a boil. Remove from heat; add couscous. Cover; stand about 5 minutes or until liquid is absorbed, fluffing with fork occasionally. Stir in butter.

3 Serve chicken mixture sprinkled with almonds on couscous.
per serving 34.1g fat; 3715kJ (889 cal)

moroccan chicken with couscous stuffing and green olive salsa

preparation time 30 minutes cooking time 2 hours 20 minutes (plus standing time) serves 4

1.6kg chicken

20g butter, melted

20 baby vine-ripened truss tomatoes (400g)

1 tablespoon olive oil

COUSCOUS STUFFING

1 teaspoon olive oil

1 medium brown onion (150g), chopped finely

1½ cups (375ml) chicken stock

¼ cup (60ml) olive oil, extra

1 tablespoon finely grated lemon rind

¼ cup (60ml) lemon juice

1 cup (200g) couscous

½ cup (70g) roasted slivered almonds

1 cup (140g) seeded dried dates, chopped finely

1 teaspoon ground cinnamon

1 teaspoon smoked paprika

1 egg, beaten lightly

GREEN OLIVE SALSA

1½ cups (180g) seeded green olives, chopped coarsely

⅓ cup (80ml) olive oil

1 tablespoon cider vinegar

1 shallot (25g), chopped finely

1 fresh long red chilli, chopped finely

¼ cup coarsely chopped fresh flat-leaf parsley

¼ cup coarsely chopped fresh mint

1 Make couscous stuffing.

2 Preheat oven to 200°C/180°C fan-forced.

3 Wash chicken under cold water; pat dry inside and out with absorbent paper. Fill large cavity loosely with couscous stuffing; tie legs together with kitchen string.

4 Half fill large baking dish with water; place chicken on oiled wire rack over dish. Brush chicken all over with butter; roast, uncovered, 15 minutes. Reduce oven temperature to 180°C/160°C fan-forced; roast, uncovered, about 1½ hours or until cooked through. Remove chicken from rack; cover, stand 20 minutes.

5 Meanwhile, place tomatoes on oven tray; drizzle with oil. Roast, uncovered, about 20 minutes or until softened and browned lightly.

6 Combine ingredients for green olive salsa in small bowl.

7 Serve chicken with tomatoes and salsa.

COUSCOUS STUFFING Heat oil in small frying pan; cook onion, stirring, until onion is soft. Combine stock, extra oil, rind and juice in medium saucepan; bring to a boil. Remove from heat. Add couscous, cover; stand about 5 minutes or until liquid is absorbed, fluffing with fork occasionally. Stir in onion, nuts, dates, spices and egg.

per serving 86.2g fat; 5518kJ (1320 cal)

spiced baby chickens with herbed yogurt

preparation time 30 minutes cooking time 20 minutes serves 4

4 x 500g chickens

2 teaspoons ground cumin

1 teaspoon ground coriander

½ teaspoon hot paprika

½ teaspoon ground tumeric

¼ teaspoon ground cinnamon

1 teaspoon salt

½ teaspoon cracked black pepper

2 tablespoons olive oil

1 medium lemon (140g), cut into wedges

HERBED YOGURT

½ teaspoon ground cumin

¼ teaspoon hot paprika

2cm piece fresh ginger (10g), grated

1 clove garlic, crushed

¼ cup finely chopped fresh coriander

¼ cup finely chopped fresh flat-leaf parsley

⅔ cup (190g) yogurt

1 Rinse chickens under cold water; pat dry inside and out with absorbent paper. Using kitchen scissors, cut along each side of each chicken's backbone; discard backbone. Place each chicken, skin-side up, on board; using heel of hand, press down on breastbone to flatten chicken.

2 Combine spices and oil in small bowl. Rub spice mixture over chickens; cook, covered, on lightly oiled grill plate (or grill or barbecue), 10 minutes. Uncover; cook 10 minutes or until chickens are cooked through.

3 Meanwhile, make herbed yogurt.

4 Serve chickens with herbed yogurt, lemon wedges and couscous, if desired.

HERBED YOGURT Dry-fry cumin and paprika in small frying pan, stirring, until fragrant. Transfer to small bowl; stir in ginger, garlic, herbs and yogurt.

per serving 51.9g fat; 2880kJ (689 cal)

lamb, lentil and spinach salad

preparation time 15 minutes cooking time 10 minutes serves 4

2 tablespoons mild curry paste
¼ cup (60ml) olive oil
600g lamb backstrap
½ teaspoon salt
1 medium brown onion (150g), chopped finely
1 large carrot (180g), chopped finely
1 trimmed celery stalk (100g), chopped finely
1 clove garlic, crushed
⅓ cup (80ml) chicken stock
400g can brown lentils, rinsed, drained
100g baby spinach leaves
½ cup loosely packed coriander leaves

1 Combine one tablespoon of curry paste and one tablespoon of oil in small bowl. Rub lamb with curry mixture then sprinkle with salt.
2 Cook lamb on heated oiled grill plate (or grill or barbecue) until browned and cooked as desired. Transfer to plate; cover, stand 5 minutes then slice thinly.
3 Meanwhile, heat remaining oil in medium pan, add onion, carrot and celery; cook, stirring, until vegetables are softened. Add garlic and remaining curry paste; cook, stirring, until fragrant.
4 Add stock and lentils; stir until hot. Remove from heat; add spinach and coriander, toss until combined.
5 Serve lamb with lentil salad.
   per serving 30.9g fat; 1998kJ (478 cal)

Harissa, a traditional spice paste used throughout North Africa, is made from dried red chillies, garlic, olive oil and caraway seeds. It can be used as a rub for meat, an ingredient in sauces and dressings, or eaten on its own as a condiment.

harissa marinated lamb with warm couscous salad

preparation time 40 minutes (plus standing and refrigeration time) **cooking time** 1 hour 5 minutes **serves** 4

30g dried red chillies, chopped coarsely

1 teaspoon ground cumin

1 teaspoon ground coriander

1 teaspoon caraway seeds

2 cloves garlic, crushed

1 teaspoon salt

1 teaspoon white sugar

⅓ cup (90g) tomato puree

⅓ cup (80ml) olive oil

2kg lamb leg

WARM COUSCOUS SALAD

2 small kumara (500g), diced into 1cm pieces

cooking-oil spray

2 cups (400g) couscous

½ cup (60g) frozen peas, thawed

1 tablespoon finely grated lemon rind

2½ cups (625ml) boiling water

1 small red onion (100g), chopped finely

½ cup finely shredded fresh flat-leaf parsley

¼ cup finely shredded fresh mint

2 tablespoons olive oil

1 tablespoon red wine vinegar

¼ cup (60ml) lemon juice

1 Place chilli in small heatproof bowl, cover with boiling water; stand 1 hour. Drain chilli; reserve ¼ cup of the soaking liquid.

2 Dry-fry cumin, coriander and caraway in heated small frying pan until fragrant. Blend or process spices with chilli, reserved soaking liquid, garlic, salt, sugar and puree until mixture is almost smooth. With motor operating, add oil in a thin, steady stream; process until harissa forms a smooth paste. Reserve ⅓ cup harissa.

3 Using sharp knife, pierce lamb all over; place in large bowl. Rub remaining harissa over lamb, pressing into cuts. Cover; refrigerate 3 hours or overnight.

4 Preheat oven to 200°C/180°C fan-forced.

5 Pour enough water into large shallow baking dish to come about 5mm up the sides; place lamb on wire rack over dish. Roast, uncovered, about 1 hour or until cooked as desired. Cover lamb; stand 20 minutes then slice thinly.

6 Meanwhile, make warm couscous salad.

7 Serve lamb with salad.

WARM COUSCOUS SALAD Place kumara, in single layer, on oiled oven tray; spray with cooking-oil spray. Roast, uncovered, for last 30 minutes of lamb cooking time. Combine couscous, peas, rind and the water in large heatproof bowl; cover, stand about 5 minutes or until water is absorbed, fluffing with fork occasionally. Stir kumara, onion, herbs and the combined olive oil, vinegar and juice into couscous salad just before serving.
per serving 49g fat; 5150kJ (1232 cal)

Preserved lemons, a prominent ingredient in North African cooking, are lemons that have been bottled in salt and lemon juice or oil for several months; their flavour is subtle and perfumed. Rinse the lemons well then remove and discard flesh, using the rind only.

grilled beef with olives and citrus couscous

preparation time 15 minutes cooking time 20 minutes serves 4

2 cloves garlic, crushed

1 teaspoon ground ginger

1 tablespoon ground cumin

2 teaspoons ground coriander

500g piece beef rump steak

1 tablespoon harissa

1 cup (250ml) beef stock

200g seeded green olives, crushed slightly

½ cup coarsely chopped fresh coriander

CITRUS COUSCOUS

2 medium oranges (480g)

1 cup (250ml) water

1 cup (250ml) orange juice

2 cups (400g) couscous

¼ cup (35g) roasted slivered almonds

1 tablespoon thinly sliced preserved lemon

1 small red onion (100g), sliced thinly

500g red radishes, trimmed, sliced thinly

1 Combine garlic and spices in medium bowl; reserve about a third of the spice mixture. Add beef to bowl with remaining spice mixture; toss to coat beef. Cook beef on heated oiled grill plate (or grill or barbecue) until cooked as desired. Cover; stand 10 minutes then slice beef thickly.

2 Make citrus couscous.

3 Meanwhile, cook harissa and remaining spice mixture in heated dry small frying pan until fragrant. Add stock; bring to a boil. Simmer, uncovered, about 3 minutes or until harissa dressing reduces by half. Remove from heat; stir in olives and coriander. Serve beef on citrus couscous; drizzle with warm harissa dressing.

CITRUS COUSCOUS Remove skin and white pith from oranges; cut in half, slice thinly. Place the water and juice in medium saucepan; bring to a boil. Remove from heat; stir in couscous. Cover; stand about 5 minutes or until liquid is absorbed, fluffing with fork occasionally. Add orange and remaining ingredients; toss gently.

per serving 15.5g fat; 3114kJ (744 cal)

kofta with tunisian carrot salad

preparation time 15 minutes cooking time 15 minutes serves 4

500g lamb mince

1 cup (70g) fresh breadcrumbs

¼ cup finely chopped fresh mint

1 teaspoon ground allspice

1 teaspoon ground coriander

1 teaspoon cracked black pepper

1 tablespoon lemon juice

⅔ cup (190g) yogurt

TUNISIAN CARROT SALAD

3 large carrots (540g)

¼ cup (60ml) lemon juice

1 tablespoon olive oil

½ teaspoon ground cinnamon

½ teaspoon ground coriander

¼ cup firmly packed fresh mint leaves

¼ cup (35g) roasted pistachios

¼ cup (40g) sultanas

1 Combine mince, breadcrumbs, mint, spices and juice in medium bowl; roll mixture into 12 balls, roll balls into sausage-shaped kofta. Cook kofta on heated oiled flat plate, uncovered, until cooked through.

2 Meanwhile, make tunisian carrot salad.

3 Serve kofta with salad and yogurt.

TUNISIAN CARROT SALAD Cut carrot into 5cm lengths then slice pieces thinly lengthways. Cook carrot on heated oiled grill plate (or grill or barbecue), uncovered, until just tender. Place in large bowl with remaining ingredients; toss gently.

per serving 20g fat; 1844kJ (441 cal)

spiced fish in banana leaves

preparation time 25 minutes cooking time 20 minutes serves 4

2 large banana leaves

¼ cup (75g) curry paste

¼ cup (60ml) water

2 tablespoons lemon juice

4 whole baby snappers (1.5kg)

6cm piece fresh ginger (30g)

4 green onions, sliced thinly

1 fresh long red chilli, chopped finely

½ cup loosely packed fresh coriander leaves

400g baby new potatoes, sliced thinly

1 Trim one banana leaf into four 25cm squares. Using tongs, dip one square at a time into large saucepan of boiling water; remove immediately. Rinse under cold water; pat dry with absorbent paper. Trim remaining banana leaf to fit grill plate.

2 Cook paste and the water, stirring, in small frying pan until fragrant. Remove from heat; stir in juice. Score fish both sides through thickest part of flesh, place in large shallow dish; brush both sides of fish with curry mixture.

3 Peel ginger; cut into small matchstick-size pieces; combine in small bowl with onion, chilli and coriander.

4 Place banana leaf squares on bench; divide potato slices among squares, overlapping slightly in centre of each leaf. Place one fish on potato on each leaf; top fish with equal amounts of the ginger mixture. Fold opposite corners of leaf over to cover fish; secure each parcel with kitchen string.

5 Place trimmed banana leaf on heated grill plate (or grill or barbecue); place fish parcels on leaf. Cook, covered, about 20 minutes or until fish is cooked as desired and potato is tender.

per serving 9.2g fat; 1372kJ (328 cal)

za'atar lamb with braised vegetables and chickpeas

preparation time 45 minutes (plus standing and refrigeration times) cooking time 40 minutes serves 4

1 cup (200g) dried chickpeas

1 bay leaf

800g lamb backstraps

¼ cup (60ml) olive oil

1 tablespoon sumac

1 tablespoon toasted sesame seeds

1 teaspoon dried thyme leaves

1 teaspoon dried oregano leaves

1 teaspoon dried marjoram leaves

1 teaspoon sweet paprika

20g butter

12 baby onions (300g), halved

1 large carrot (180g), chopped finely

2 trimmed celery stalks (200g), chopped finely

2 small fennel bulbs (400g), trimmed, sliced thinly

1 cup firmly packed fresh flat-leaf parsley leaves

SUMAC DRESSING

1 tablespoon sumac

1 teaspoon dijon mustard

¼ cup (60ml) olive oil

¼ cup (60ml) lemon juice

1 Place chickpeas in large bowl of cold water; stand overnight. Drain.

2 Cook chickpeas and bay leaf in medium saucepan of boiling water, uncovered, until just tender; drain. Rinse under cold water; drain.

3 Meanwhile, place lamb, 2 tablespoons of the oil and combined sumac, seeds, dried herbs and paprika in large bowl; toss to coat lamb. Cover; refrigerate 30 minutes.

4 Meanwhile, combine ingredients for sumac dressing in screw-top jar; shake well.

5 Heat butter and remaining oil in large frying pan; cook onion, stirring, about 10 minutes or until browned lightly and softened. Add carrot, celery and fennel; cook, stirring, until vegetables are just tender.

6 Meanwhile, cook lamb, in batches, on heated oiled grill plate (or grill or barbecue) until browned and cooked as desired. Cover; stand 5 minutes then slice lamb thickly.

7 Just before serving, combine chickpeas, parsley and half the dressing with vegetables; cook, stirring, until heated through. Divide chickpea salad among serving plates; top with lamb, drizzle with remaining dressing.
per serving 47.9g fat; 3194kJ (763 cal)

spice-rubbed beef fillet with chickpea and preserved lemon salad

preparation time 20 minutes (plus refrigeration time) cooking time 15 minutes serves 4

1 teaspoon coriander seeds

1 teaspoon kalonji seeds

1 teaspoon dried chilli flakes

1 teaspoon sea salt

1 clove garlic, crushed

600g piece beef eye fillet, trimmed

6 large egg tomatoes (540g), peeled

425g can chickpeas, rinsed, drained

2 tablespoons finely chopped preserved lemon rind

⅔ cup loosely packed fresh flat-leaf parsley leaves

⅔ cup loosely packed fresh coriander leaves

1 tablespoon lemon juice

1 Using mortar and pestle, crush seeds, chilli, salt and garlic into coarse paste; rub paste into beef. Cover; refrigerate 20 minutes.

2 Meanwhile, quarter tomatoes; discard seeds and pulp. Chop tomato flesh finely. Combine in medium bowl with chickpeas, rind, herbs and juice.

3 Cook beef on lightly oiled heated grill plate (or grill or barbecue) until browned all over and cooked as desired. Cover; stand 10 minutes then slice thinly. Serve beef on salad.

per serving 8g fat; 1166kJ (279 cal)

moroccan fish fillets

preparation time 20 minutes cooking time 15 minutes serves 4

1 clove garlic, crushed

1cm piece fresh ginger (5g), grated

1 teaspoon ground cumin

½ teaspoon ground turmeric

½ teaspoon hot paprika

½ teaspoon ground coriander

4 x 200g fish fillets, skinned

1 tablespoon olive oil

FRUITY COUSCOUS

2 cups (400g) couscous

2 cups (500ml) boiling water

50g butter

1 large pear (330g), chopped finely

½ cup (80g) finely chopped dried apricots

½ cup (95g) coarsely chopped dried figs

½ cup coarsely chopped fresh flat-leaf parsley

¼ cup (40g) roasted pine nuts

1   Combine garlic, ginger and spices in large bowl. Add fish; toss to coat fish in spice mixture. Heat oil in large frying pan; cook fish, in batches, until browned both sides and cooked as desired.

2   Meanwhile, make fruity couscous.

3   Divide couscous among serving plates; top with fish. Accompany with a bowl of combined yogurt and coarsely chopped fresh coriander, if desired.
FRUITY COUSCOUS Combine couscous, the water and butter in large heatproof bowl, cover; stand about 5 minutes or until liquid is absorbed, fluffing with fork occasionally. Stir in remaining ingredients.
per serving 27.5g fat; 3816kJ (912 cal)

Traditional to North Africa, a tagine is an aromatic
casseroled stew, traditionally cooked and served
in an earthenware dish also called a tagine.

beef and prune tagine

preparation time 20 minutes cooking time 2 hours 30 minutes serves 4

2 large red onions (600g), chopped finely

2 tablespoons olive oil

1 teaspoon cracked black pepper

pinch saffron threads

1 teaspoon ground cinnamon

¼ teaspoon ground ginger

1kg beef blade steak, diced into 4cm pieces

50g butter, chopped

425g can diced tomatoes

1 cup (250ml) water

2 tablespoons white sugar

¾ cup (100g) roasted slivered almonds

1½ cups (250g) seeded prunes

1 teaspoon finely grated lemon rind

¼ teaspoon ground cinnamon, extra

SPINACH COUSCOUS

1½ cups (300g) couscous

1½ cups (375ml) boiling water

80g finely shredded baby spinach leaves

1 Combine onion, oil and spices in large bowl, add beef; toss beef to coat in mixture.
2 Place beef in large deep saucepan with butter, undrained tomatoes, the water, half the sugar and ½ cup of the nuts; bring to a boil. Simmer, covered, 1½ hours. Remove 1 cup cooking liquid; reserve. Simmer tagine, uncovered, 30 minutes.
3 Meanwhile, place prunes in small bowl, cover with boiling water; stand 20 minutes, drain. Place prunes in small saucepan with rind, extra cinnamon, remaining sugar and reserved cooking liquid; bring to a boil. Reduce heat; simmer, uncovered, about 15 minutes or until prunes soften. Stir into tagine.
4 Make spinach couscous.
5 Divide couscous and tagine among serving plates; sprinkle tagine with remaining nuts.
   SPINACH COUSCOUS Combine couscous and the water in large heatproof bowl, cover; stand about 5 minutes or until water is absorbed, fluffing with fork occasionally. Stir in spinach.
   per serving 50.3g fat; 4799kJ (1148 cal)

TAGINES & STEWS

chicken, olive and preserved lemon tagine

preparation time 30 minutes (plus standing time) cooking time 2 hours 30 minutes serves 8

1 cup (200g) dried chickpeas

2 tablespoons plain flour

2 teaspoons hot paprika

8 chicken drumsticks (1.2kg)

8 chicken thigh cutlets (1.6kg)

40g butter

2 medium red onions (340g), sliced thickly

3 cloves garlic, crushed

1 teaspoon cumin seeds

½ teaspoon ground turmeric

½ teaspoon ground coriander

¼ teaspoon saffron threads

1 teaspoon dried chilli flakes

1 teaspoon ground ginger

3 cups (750ml) chicken stock

2 tablespoons finely sliced preserved lemon rind

⅓ cup (40g) seeded green olives

2 tablespoons finely chopped fresh coriander

TUNISIAN-STYLE RICE

3 cups (600g) white long-grain rice

20g butter

1.5 litres (6 cups) water

1 Place chickpeas in medium bowl, cover with water; stand overnight, drain. Rinse under cold water; drain. Place chickpeas in medium saucepan of boiling water; return to a boil. Simmer, uncovered, about 40 minutes or until chickpeas are tender.

2 Preheat oven to 160°C/140°C fan-forced.

3 Place flour and paprika in plastic bag, add chicken, in batches; shake gently to coat chicken in flour mixture.

4 Melt butter in large flameproof casserole dish; cook chicken pieces, in batches, until browned. Cook onion in same dish, stirring, until softened. Add garlic, cumin, turmeric, ground coriander, saffron, chilli and ginger; cook, stirring, until fragrant.

5 Return chicken with stock to dish; bring to a boil then cook, covered, in oven 30 minutes. Add drained chickpeas; cook tagine, covered, in oven 1 hour.

6 Meanwhile, make tunisian-style rice.

7 Remove tagine from oven. Stir in lemon, olives and fresh coriander just before serving with rice.

TUNISIAN-STYLE RICE Wash rice in strainer under cold water until water runs clear; drain. Melt butter in large saucepan, add rice; stir until rice is coated in butter. Add the water; bring to a boil. Simmer rice, partially covered, about 10 minutes or until steam holes appear on surface. Cover rice tightly, reduce heat to as low as possible; steam 10 minutes (do not remove lid). Remove from heat; stand 10 minutes without removing lid. Fluff with fork before serving.

per serving 35.5g fat; 3377kJ (807 cal)

chickpea and vegetable tagine

preparation time 15 minutes cooking time 20 minutes serves 4

2 tablespoons olive oil

2 large brown onions (400g), sliced thickly

2 cloves garlic, crushed

2 teaspoons ground coriander

1 teaspoon ground cumin

1 teaspoon sweet paprika

2 cinnamon sticks

pinch ground saffron

2 fresh small red chillies, chopped coarsely

2 baby eggplants (120g), chopped coarsely

800g peeled pumpkin, chopped coarsely

400g can chopped tomatoes

1 cup (250ml) vegetable stock

2 cups (500ml) water

200g can chickpeas, rinsed, drained

2 large zucchini (300g), chopped coarsely

½ cup fresh coriander leaves

1 tablespoon lemon juice

COUSCOUS

1 cup (250ml) vegetable stock

1 cup (250ml) water

60g butter

1½ cups (300g) couscous

1   Heat oil in large deep frying pan; cook onion and garlic, stirring, until onion softens. Add spices, chilli and eggplant; cook, stirring, until fragrant.

2   Add pumpkin, undrained tomatoes, stock, the water and chickpeas; bring to a boil. Simmer, covered, 10 minutes. Add zucchini; simmer, covered, 5 minutes or until vegetables are tender.

3   Meanwhile, make couscous.

4   Stir coriander and lemon juice into vegetable mixture; serve with couscous.

COUSCOUS Place stock, the water and butter in large saucepan; bring to a boil. Stir in couscous, remove from heat; stand, covered, about 5 minutes or until liquid is absorbed, fluffing with fork occasionally.

per serving 24.4g fat; 2750kJ (658 cal)

Chicken tagine can be made three hours ahead and stored, covered, in the refrigerator. The tagine is also suitable to freeze, without the nuts and coriander.

chicken tagine with dates and honey

preparation time 25 minutes cooking time 1 hour 45 minutes serves 4

1kg chicken thigh fillets

2 tablespoons olive oil

2 medium brown onions (300g), sliced thinly

4 cloves garlic, crushed

1 teaspoon cumin seeds

1 teaspoon ground coriander

1 teaspoon ground ginger

1 teaspoon ground turmeric

1 teaspoon ground cinnamon

½ teaspoon chilli powder

¼ teaspoon ground nutmeg

1½ cups (375ml) chicken stock

1 cup (250ml) water

½ cup (70g) seedless dates, halved

¼ cup (90g) honey

½ cup (80g) roasted blanched almonds

1 tablespoon coarsely chopped fresh coriander

1 Cut chicken into 3cm strips. Heat 1 tablespoon of the oil in medium saucepan; cook chicken, in batches, stirring, until browned. Drain on absorbent paper.

2 Heat remaining oil in same pan, add onion, garlic and spices; cook, stirring, until onion is soft.

3 Return chicken to pan with stock and the water; simmer, covered, 1 hour. Remove lid; simmer about 30 minutes or until mixture is thickened slightly and chicken is tender. Stir in dates, honey and nuts; sprinkle with coriander.
per serving 40.2g fat; 2855kJ (683 cal)

lamb and apricot tagine

preparation time 20 minutes (plus standing time) cooking time 1 hour serves 8

1⅔ cups (250g) dried apricots

¾ cup (180ml) orange juice

½ cup (125ml) boiling water

2 tablespoons olive oil

900g diced lamb

2 medium red capsicums (400g), chopped coarsely

1 large brown onion (200g), chopped coarsely

2 medium kumara (800g), chopped coarsely

3 cloves garlic, crushed

1 teaspoon ground cinnamon

2 teaspoons ground cumin

2 teaspoons ground coriander

1 cup (250ml) dry red wine

1 litre (4 cups) chicken stock

2 tablespoons honey

1 cup loosely packed fresh coriander leaves

¾ cup (200g) low-fat yogurt

CITRUS COUSCOUS

1 litre (4 cups) water

4 cups (800g) couscous

1 tablespoon finely grated orange rind

2 teaspoons finely grated lemon rind

2 teaspoons finely grated lime rind

1 Combine apricots, juice and the water in small bowl. Cover; stand 45 minutes.

2 Meanwhile, heat half the oil in large saucepan; cook lamb, in batches, until browned all over.

3 Heat remaining oil in same pan; cook capsicum, onion, kumara, garlic and ground spices, stirring, until onion softens and mixture is fragrant. Add wine, bring to a boil; simmer, uncovered, about 5 minutes or until liquid reduces by half.

4 Return lamb to pan with undrained apricots, stock and honey; bring to a boil. Simmer, covered, about 50 minutes or until lamb is tender. Remove from heat; stir in fresh coriander.

5 Meanwhile, make citrus couscous.

6 Serve lamb and apricot tagine on citrus couscous; drizzle with yogurt.
   CITRUS COUSCOUS Bring the water to a boil in medium saucepan; stir in couscous and rinds. Remove from heat; stand, covered, about 5 minutes or until water is absorbed, fluffing with fork occasionally.
   per serving 12.8g fat; 1837kJ (439 cal)

slow-cooked lamb shanks with sweet potato

preparation time 20 minutes cooking time 2 hours 55 minutes serves 4

8 french-trimmed lamb shanks (2kg)

2 tablespoons plain flour

¼ cup (60ml) olive oil

2 medium brown onions (300g), chopped coarsely

3 cloves garlic, crushed

1 teaspoon ground cinnamon

2 teaspoons ground cumin

2 teaspoons ground coriander

1 cup (250ml) dry red wine

1 litre (4 cups) chicken stock

2 tablespoons honey

2 small sweet potatoes (500g), chopped coarsely

OLIVE AND ALMOND COUSCOUS

1½ cups (300g) couscous

1½ cups (375ml) boiling water

20g butter

2 tablespoons finely chopped preserved lemon

¾ cup (90g) seeded green olives, chopped coarsely

⅓ cup coarsely chopped fresh flat-leaf parsley

⅓ cup (45g) roasted slivered almonds

1 medium green capsicum (200g), chopped finely

1 Preheat oven to 180°C/160°C fan-forced.

2 Toss lamb in flour; shake away excess. Heat 2 tablespoons of the oil in large flameproof casserole dish; cook lamb, in batches, until browned all over. Drain on absorbent paper.

3 Heat remaining oil in same dish; cook onion, garlic, cinnamon, cumin and coriander, stirring, until onion softens and mixture is fragrant. Add wine; bring to a boil. Simmer, uncovered, about 5 minutes or until liquid reduces by half.

4 Add stock and honey to same dish; bring to a boil. Return lamb to casserole dish; cook, covered, in oven, about 1½ hours, turning shanks occasionally. Uncover dish, add sweet potato; return to oven. Cook, uncovered, about 50 minutes or until potato is just tender and lamb is almost falling off the bone. Transfer lamb and potato to platter; cover to keep warm.

5 Place dish with pan juices over high heat; bring to a boil. Boil, uncovered, about 15 minutes or until sauce thickens slightly.

6 Meanwhile, make olive and almond couscous.

7 Serve shanks with couscous.

OLIVE AND ALMOND COUSCOUS Combine couscous with the water and butter in large heatproof bowl, cover; stand about 5 minutes or until liquid is absorbed, fluffing with fork occasionally. Stir in remaining ingredients.

per serving 38.1g fat; 4339kJ (1038 cal)

lamb and quince tagine with pistachio couscous

preparation time 20 minutes cooking time 1 hour 30 minutes serves 4

40g butter

600g diced lamb

1 medium red onion (170g), chopped coarsely

2 cloves garlic, crushed

1 cinnamon stick

2 teaspoons ground coriander

1 teaspoon ground cumin

1 teaspoon ground ginger

1 teaspoon dried chilli flakes

1½ cups (375ml) water

425g can crushed tomatoes

2 medium quinces (700g), peeled, cored, quartered

1 large zucchini (150g), chopped coarsely

2 tablespoons coarsely chopped fresh coriander

PISTACHIO COUSCOUS

1½ cups (300g) couscous

1 cup (250ml) boiling water

20g butter, softened

½ cup finely chopped fresh coriander

¼ cup (35g) roasted pistachios, chopped coarsely

1 Melt butter in large saucepan; cook lamb, in batches, until browned. Add onion to same pan; cook, stirring, until softened. Add garlic, cinnamon, ground coriander, cumin, ginger and chilli; cook, stirring, until mixture is fragrant.

2 Return lamb to pan. Stir in the water, undrained tomatoes and quince; bring to a boil. Simmer, covered, 30 minutes. Uncover; simmer, stirring occasionally, about 1 hour or until quince is rosy and tender and sauce has thickened.

3 Add zucchini; cook, stirring, about 10 minutes or until zucchini is just tender.

4 Meanwhile, make pistachio couscous.

5 Serve couscous with tagine; sprinkle with coriander.

PISTACHIO COUSCOUS Combine couscous with the water and butter in large heatproof bowl, cover; stand about 5 minutes or until liquid is absorbed, fluffing with fork occasionally. Stir in coriander and nuts.

per serving 31g fat; 3214kJ (769 cal)

chicken, cinnamon and prune tagine

preparation time 20 minutes cooking time 1 hour 30 minutes serves 8

2 tablespoons olive oil

2kg chicken thigh fillets

3 teaspoons cumin seeds

3 teaspoons ground coriander

1 tablespoon smoked paprika

3 teaspoons ground cumin

4 cinnamon sticks

4 medium brown onions (600g), sliced thinly

8 cloves garlic, crushed

3 cups (750ml) chicken stock

1 cup (250ml) dry red wine

1 cup (170g) seeded prunes

½ cup (80g) roasted blanched almonds

¼ cup coarsely chopped fresh flat-leaf parsley

1 Heat half the oil in large saucepan; cook chicken, in batches, until browned.
2 Meanwhile, dry-fry spices in small heated frying pan, stirring, until fragrant.
3 Heat remaining oil in same saucepan; cook onion and garlic, stirring, until onion softens. Return chicken to pan with spices, stock and wine; bring to a boil. Simmer, covered, 40 minutes.
4 Stir in prunes; simmer, uncovered, about 20 minutes or until chicken is tender. Stir in nuts and parsley.
per serving 28.8g fat; 2236kJ (535 cal)

pumpkin and bean tagine
with harissa and almond couscous

preparation time 30 minutes cooking time 30 minutes serves 6

20g butter

1 tablespoon olive oil

2 medium brown onions (300g), chopped coarsely

2 cloves garlic, crushed

4cm piece fresh ginger (20g), grated

2 teaspoons ground cumin

2 teaspoons ground coriander

2 teaspoons finely grated lemon rind

1kg pumpkin, chopped coarsely

400g can chopped tomatoes

2 cups (500ml) vegetable stock

400g green beans, cut into 5cm lengths

⅓ cup (55g) sultanas

1 tablespoon honey

¼ cup finely chopped fresh flat-leaf parsley

¼ cup finely chopped fresh mint

HARISSA AND ALMOND COUSCOUS

2 cups (500ml) vegetable stock

1 cup (250ml) water

3 cups (600g) couscous

½ cup (70g) roasted slivered almonds

1 tablespoon harissa

1   Heat butter and oil in large saucepan; cook onion and garlic, stirring, 5 minutes. Add ginger, spices and rind; cook about 1 minute or until fragrant. Add pumpkin, undrained tomatoes and stock; bring to a boil. Simmer, covered, about 15 minutes or until pumpkin is just tender.

2   Meanwhile, make harissa and almond couscous.

3   Add beans to tagine mixture; cook, stirring, 5 minutes. Stir sultanas, honey and chopped herbs through tagine off the heat just before serving with couscous.

HARISSA AND ALMOND COUSCOUS Bring stock and the water to a boil in medium saucepan; remove from heat. Add couscous; cover, stand about 5 minutes or until liquid is absorbed, fluffing with fork occasionally. Gently mix nuts and harissa through couscous.

per serving 14.4g fat; 2668kJ (637 cal)

quince and chicken tagine

preparation time 25 minutes cooking time 1 hour 50 minutes serves 4

2 medium quinces (700g), peeled, cored, cut into wedges

40g butter

⅓ cup (115g) honey

3 cups (750ml) water

2 teaspoons orange flower water

2 teaspoons olive oil

4 chicken drumsticks (600g)

4 chicken thigh cutlets (800g), skin removed

1 large brown onion (200g), chopped coarsely

3 cloves garlic, crushed

1 teaspoon ground cumin

1 teaspoon ground ginger

pinch saffron threads

2 cups (500ml) chicken stock

2 large zucchini (300g), chopped coarsely

¼ cup coarsely chopped fresh coriander

CORIANDER COUSCOUS

1½ cups (300g) couscous

1½ cups (375ml) boiling water

50g baby spinach leaves, chopped finely

2 green onions, sliced thinly

2 tablespoons finely chopped fresh coriander

1 Place quince, butter, honey, the water and orange flower water in medium saucepan; bring to a boil. Simmer, covered, 1 hour, stirring occasionally. Uncover; cook, stirring occasionally, about 45 minutes or until quince is rosy and tender.

2 Meanwhile, heat oil in large frying pan; cook chicken, in batches, until browned. Cook onion, garlic and spices in same pan, stirring, until onion softens. Return chicken to pan with stock; bring to a boil then simmer, covered, 20 minutes. Uncover; simmer, about 20 minutes or until chicken is cooked though. Add zucchini; cook, uncovered, about 10 minutes or until zucchini is tender. Stir in quince and ½ cup of the quince syrup.

3 Meanwhile, make coriander couscous.

4 Divide tagine and couscous among serving plates; sprinkle tagine with coriander.

CORIANDER COUSCOUS Combine couscous with the water in large heatproof bowl; cover, stand about 5 minutes or until water is absorbed, fluffing with fork occasionally. Stir in spinach, onion and coriander.

per serving 32.6g fat; 3913kJ (936 cal)

lamb and okra in rich tomato sauce with spiced garlic

preparation time 20 minutes cooking time 2 hours 10 minutes serves 4

1 tablespoon olive oil

1kg boned lamb shoulder, trimmed, chopped coarsely

2 medium brown onions (300g), chopped coarsely

7 medium tomatoes (1kg), chopped coarsely

1 litre (4 cups) water

200g okra

½ cup loosely packed fresh mint leaves

SPICED GARLIC

1 teaspoon coriander seeds

½ teaspoon cardamom seeds

30g butter

5 cloves garlic, sliced thinly

1 teaspoon dried chilli flakes

1 teaspoon salt

1 Heat oil in large deep saucepan; cook lamb, in batches, until browned all over.

2 Cook onion in same pan, stirring, until soft. Add tomato and the water; bring to a boil. Return lamb to pan; simmer, uncovered, stirring occasionally, about 1¾ hours or until lamb is tender.

3 Add okra to lamb mixture; simmer, uncovered, about 15 minutes or until okra is tender.

4 Meanwhile, make spiced garlic.

5 Serve casserole with spiced garlic, mint and steamed white long-grain rice, if desired.

SPICED GARLIC Using mortar and pestle, crush seeds. Melt butter in small saucepan; cook seeds, garlic, chilli and salt over low heat, stirring, about 10 minutes or until garlic softens.

per serving 33.5g fat; 2286kJ (547 cal)

fish and tomato tagine

preparation time 20 minutes cooking time 40 minutes serves 4

2 tablespoons olive oil

2 large brown onions (400g), chopped coarsely

6 cloves garlic, chopped finely

1 fresh small red chilli, chopped finely

4 drained anchovy fillets, chopped finely

¾ cup coarsely chopped fresh flat-leaf parsley

1 cup coarsely chopped fresh coriander

¾ cup coarsely chopped fresh mint

200g mushrooms, quartered

2 trimmed celery stalks (200g), sliced thickly

2 teaspoons ground cumin

2 x 425g cans diced tomatoes

4 fish cutlets (1kg)

1 medium lemon (140g), cut into wedges

2 tablespoons fresh flat-leaf parsley leaves

TOMATO AND HERB SALAD

5 medium tomatoes (750g), coarsely chopped

2 tablespoons coarsely chopped fresh mint

¼ cup coarsely chopped fresh flat-leaf parsley

2 tablespoons coarsely chopped fresh dill

2 cloves crushed garlic

2 tablespoons lemon juice

1 tablespoon olive oil

2 teaspoons white vinegar

1 Preheat oven to 200°C/180°C fan-forced.
2 Heat oil in large deep flameproof baking dish; cook onion, garlic and chilli, stirring, until onion softens. Add anchovy, chopped herbs, mushrooms, celery and cumin; cook, stirring, 5 minutes.
3 Add undrained tomatoes; bring to a boil. Add fish; submerge it in tomato mixture. Return to a boil then cook, uncovered, in oven about 20 minutes or until liquid has almost evaporated and fish is cooked as desired.
4 Meanwhile, make tomato and herb salad.
5 Divide fish and lemon wedges among serving plates; sprinkle with parsley leaves. Serve with salad and, if desired, steamed white long-grain rice.
   TOMATO AND HERB SALAD Combine tomatoes and herbs in medium bowl, drizzle with combined garlic, juice, oil and vinegar; toss gently.
   per serving 20.9g fat; 2161kJ (517 cal)

fresh peaches and dates with orange flower water

preparation time 10 minutes (plus refrigeration time) cooking time 5 minutes serves 8

½ cup (125ml) water

½ cup (125ml) caster sugar

pinch saffron threads

4 cardamom pods

⅓ cup (80ml) lemon juice

1 teaspoon orange flower water

6 large peaches (1.5kg), sliced thickly

12 fresh dates (250g), quartered

1 cup (280g) yogurt

1 Combine the water, sugar, saffron and cardamom in small saucepan; stir over low heat, without boiling, until sugar is dissolved. Bring to boil; simmer, uncovered, about 5 minutes or until mixture just thickens. Cool 10 minutes. Stir in juice and orange flower water.

2 Place peaches and dates in large bowl; strain syrup over fruit. Refrigerate 2 hours.

3 Serve fruit with yogurt.
per serving 2.7g fat; 811kJ (194 cal)

DESSERTS & TEAS

poached nectarines with orange almond bread

preparation time 25 minutes cooking time 1 hour 20 minutes (plus refrigeration and cooling time) serves 4

3 cups (750g) water

1 cup (220g) caster sugar

1 star anise

10cm strip orange rind

8 small nectarines (800g)

⅔ cup (190g) yogurt

ORANGE ALMOND BREAD

2 egg whites

⅓ cup (75g) caster sugar

¾ cup (110g) plain flour

1 teaspoon finely grated orange rind

¾ cup (120g) blanched almonds

1   Make orange almond bread.
2   Combine the water, sugar, star anise and rind in medium saucepan, stir over medium heat until sugar dissolves; bring to a boil. Boil, uncovered, 2 minutes. Add nectarines; simmer, uncovered, 20 minutes. Cool nectarines 10 minutes in poaching liquid.
3   Using slotted spoon, transfer nectarines to serving dishes; bring liquid to a boil. Boil, uncovered, about 5 minutes or until syrup reduces to 1 cup; strain into small bowl.
4   Cool syrup to room temperature; pour ¼ cup of the syrup over nectarines in each dish; serve with yogurt and orange almond bread.
ORANGE ALMOND BREAD Preheat oven to 180°C/160°C fan-forced. Grease and line 8cm x 25cm bar cake pan. Beat egg whites in small bowl with electric mixer until soft peaks form. Gradually add sugar, 1 tablespoon at a time, beating until sugar dissolves between additions; transfer to medium bowl. Gently fold in flour, rind and nuts; spread into pan. Bake, uncovered, about 30 minutes or until browned lightly; cool in pan. Wrap in foil; refrigerate 3 hours or overnight. Preheat oven to 150°C/130°C fan-forced. Using serrated knife, cut bread into 3mm slices; place slices on baking-paper-lined oven trays. Bake, uncovered, about 15 minutes or until crisp.
per serving 20.6g fat; 2867kJ (686 cal)

honey-grilled plums and figs

preparation time 5 minutes cooking time 8 minutes serves 4

8 small plums (600g), halved, stoned

6 medium figs (360g), halved

⅓ cup (115g) honey

2 tablespoons brown sugar

⅔ cup (190g) yogurt

1 Preheat grill.
2 Place plums and figs on shallow baking tray; drizzle with half the honey, sprinkle with sugar. Grill until browned lightly and just tender.
3 Divide fruit among serving plates, drizzle with remaining honey and juices in baking tray. Serve with yogurt.
   per serving 3.7g fat; 1124kJ (269 cal)

baked rice pudding with poached quince

preparation time 20 minutes cooking time 2 hours 20 minutes serves 4

1.25 litres (5 cups) water

1kg (5 cups) caster sugar

4 medium quinces (1.5kg), peeled,
cored, quartered

10cm strip lemon rind

1 tablespoon lemon juice

1 cinnamon stick, halved

½ cup (100g) calrose medium-grain rice

2¾ cups (680ml) milk

300ml cream

⅓ cup (75g) caster sugar, extra

1 teaspoon vanilla extract

½ cup (75g) vienna almonds, chopped coarsely

1 Combine the water and sugar in large pan; stir over medium heat without boiling, until sugar dissolves; bring to a boil. Add quince, rind, juice and half cinnamon stick; simmer, covered, about 2 hours or until quince are rosy and tender.

2 Preheat oven to 150°C/130°C fan-forced.

3 Place rice in sieve; rinse under cold water until water runs clear, drain.

4 Place rice, milk, cream, extra sugar, extract and remaining half cinnamon stick in small baking dish; stir. Bake, uncovered, about 2 hours or until tender, stirring every 30 minutes.

5 Serve rice with quince and a little of the syrup; sprinkle with nuts.
per serving 46.5g fat; 8159kJ (1952 cal)

Known variously throughout the Middle East and North Africa as basboosa, namoura or harisi, this sweet slice is saturated with a citrusy sugar syrup.

semolina slice

preparation time 15 minutes cooking time 1 hour 50 minutes (plus cooling and refrigeration time) makes 28

1kg (6¼ cups) coarsely ground semolina

2½ cups (550g) white sugar

1 cup (250ml) milk

125g butter

¼ cup (40g) blanched almonds

SUGAR SYRUP

3 cups (750ml) water

2 teaspoons lemon juice

1½ cups (330g) caster sugar

2 teaspoons orange flower water

1 Make sugar syrup.
2 Preheat oven to 160°C/140°C fan-forced. Grease 20cm x 30cm lamington pan.
3 Combine semolina and sugar in large bowl. Combine milk and butter in small saucepan; stir over low heat until butter melts. Pour into semolina mixture; stir to combine.
4 Spread mixture into pan; smooth top. Score slice into 4cm diamond shapes; centre one nut on each diamond. Bake, uncovered, in oven about 1 hour 20 minutes or until slice is golden brown and slightly firm to the touch.
5 Cut through diamond shapes to bottom of slice; gradually pour cooled syrup over hot slice. Cool slice in pan.
   SUGAR SYRUP Combine the water, juice and sugar in medium saucepan; bring to a boil. Simmer, uncovered, about 20 minutes or until syrup reduces to about 2½ cups. Cool to room temperature. Add orange flower water, cover; refrigerate 3 hours or overnight. (Syrup is best made the day before, covered and refrigerated; remove from refrigerator when slice goes into the oven so that syrup is at room temperature before pouring over hot slice.)
   per piece 5.2g fat; 1182kJ (282 cal)

poached plums with almond milk ice-cream

preparation time 20 minutes **cooking time** 40 minutes (plus standing, refrigeration and freezing time) **serves** 4

2 cups (500ml) water

½ cup (70g) roasted slivered almonds

1 vanilla bean

300ml cream

¾ cup (165g) caster sugar

6 egg yolks

POACHED PLUMS

2 cups (500ml) water

1 cup (250ml) port

½ cup (110g) caster sugar

1 cinnamon stick

4 plums (450g), halved, stoned

1 Line 14cm x 21cm loaf pan with baking paper.

2 Blend or process the water and nuts until fine. Strain almond milk through muslin-lined strainer into medium saucepan; discard solids.

3 Halve vanilla bean lengthways, scrape seeds into pan with almond milk. Add pod, cream and ¼ cup of the sugar to pan; bring to a boil. Remove from heat; stand 30 minutes. Discard pod.

4 Beat egg yolks and remaining sugar in medium bowl with electric mixer until thick and creamy. Gradually stir in almond milk mixture; return to pan. Cook, stirring, over low heat, until mixture thickens slightly. Remove from heat; cool to room temperature. Pour ice-cream mixture into loaf pan, cover with foil; freeze until firm.

5 Remove ice-cream from freezer, turn into large bowl; chop ice-cream coarsely then beat with electric mixer until smooth. Return to loaf pan, cover; freeze until firm.

6 Meanwhile, make poached plums.

7 Cut ice-cream into four slices; divide among serving plates. Top with plums and syrup.

POACHED PLUMS Stir the water, port, sugar and cinnamon in medium saucepan, without boiling, until sugar dissolves. Add plums; cook, uncovered, over low heat, about 30 minutes or until just tender. Remove plums from syrup; discard skins. Bring syrup to a boil; boil, uncovered, about 10 minutes or until syrup is reduced to about 1 cup. Remove from heat, discard cinnamon; cool 10 minutes. Refrigerate, covered, until cold.

per serving 46.7g fat; 3563kJ (851 cal)

spiced lemon tea

preparation time 5 minutes cooking time 5 minutes (plus refrigeration time) makes 3 litres (12 cups)

1 litre (4 cups) water

4 tea bags

1 cinnamon stick

2 cardamom pods

4 whole cloves

1 cup (220g) caster sugar

1½ cups (375ml) cold water, extra

½ cup (125ml) fresh lemon juice

2 cups (500ml) fresh orange juice

1 medium lemon (140g), sliced thinly

¼ cup coarsely chopped fresh mint

1 litre (4 cups) mineral water

ice cubes

1 Bring the water to a boil in large saucepan; add tea bags, spices and sugar. Stir over low heat about 3 minutes or until sugar is dissolved; discard tea bags. Refrigerate until cold.

2 Discard spices then stir in the extra water, juices, lemon and mint. Just before serving, add mineral water and ice cubes.
   per 250ml 0.1g fat; 376kJ (90 cal)

moroccan mint tea

preparation time 10 minutes (plus refrigeration time) makes 1 litre (4 cups)

1 litre (4 cups) hot water

3 tea bags

1 cup loosely packed fresh mint leaves

2 tablespoons caster sugar

½ cup loosely packed fresh mint leaves, extra

1 cup ice cubes

1 Combine the water, tea bags, mint and sugar in medium heatproof jug, stand 10 minutes; discard tea bags. Cover; refrigerate until cool.

2 Strain tea mixture; discard leaves. Stir in extra mint and ice cubes; serve immediately.
   per 250ml 0.2g fat; 176kJ (42 cal)

ALLSPICE also known as jamaican pepper or pimento; so-named because it tastes like a combination of nutmeg, cumin, clove and cinnamon. Available whole (a dark-brown berry the size of a pea) or ground, and used in both sweet and savoury dishes.

ALMONDS flat, pointy-tipped nuts having a pitted brown shell enclosing a creamy white kernel that is covered by a brown skin.
blanched brown skins removed.
meal also known as ground almonds; nuts are powdered to a coarse flour texture for use in baking or as a thickening agent.
slivered small pieces cut lengthways.
vienna toffee-coated almonds.

BANANA LEAVES can be ordered from fruit and vegetable stores. Cut with a sharp knife close to the main stem then immerse in hot water so leaves will be pliable. Foil can be used if banana leaves are unavailable.

BASIL an aromatic herb; there are many types of basil, and the appearance of the leaves and scent varies, but the most commonly used basil in cooking is sweet basil.

BAY LEAF aromatic leaves from the bay tree used to flavour soups, stocks and casseroles.

BEANS
green also known as french or string beans (although the tough string they once had has generally been bred out of them), this long thin fresh bean is consumed in its entirety once cooked.
butter also known as lima beans; large, flat, kidney-shaped bean, off-white in colour, with a mealy texture and mild taste. Available canned and dried.
lima *see beans, butter.*

BEEF EYE FILLET a tenderloin fillet with a fine, extremely tender texture. Is one of the most expensive cuts of beef.

BEETROOT also known as red beets or just beets; a firm, round root vegetable.

BREAD
pitta also known as lebanese bread; wheat-flour pocket bread sold in large, flat pieces that separate into two thin rounds. *Pocket pitta,* smaller, thicker pieces, are also available.
ciabatta a crisp-crusted, open-textured white sourdough bread.

BREADCRUMBS, FRESH fresh bread, usually white, processed into crumbs; good for poultry stuffing and as a thickening agent in some soups and cold sauces.

BURGHUL also known as bulghur wheat; hulled steamed wheat kernels that, once dried, are crushed into various size grains. It is not the same thing as cracked wheat.

BUTTER use salted or unsalted (sweet) butter; 125g is equal to one stick of butter.

CAPERS the grey-green buds of a warm climate (usually Mediterranean) shrub, sold either dried and salted or pickled in a vinegar brine; tiny young ones, called *baby capers,* are also available both in brine or dried in salt. Must be rinsed well before using.

CAPSICUM also known as pepper or bell pepper. Native to Central and South America; found in red, green, yellow, purplish-black and orange varieties. Seeds and membranes should be discarded before use.

CARAWAY SEEDS small, half-moon-shaped dried seeds from a member of the parsley family; adds a sharp anise flavour when used in both sweet and savoury dishes.

CARDAMOM can be purchased in pod, seed or ground form. Has a distinctive aromatic, sweetly rich flavour and is one of the world's most expensive spices.

CASHEWS plump, kidney-shaped, golden-brown nuts having a distinctive sweet, buttery flavour; they have a high fat content, so should be kept, sealed tightly, under refrigeration to avoid becoming rancid. We use roasted unsalted cashews in this book, available from most supermarkets.

CAYENNE PEPPER *see chilli.*

CHICKEN
breast fillet breast halved, skinned and boned.
drumette small fleshy part of the wing between shoulder and elbow; trimmed to resemble a drumstick.
drumstick leg with skin and bone intact.
maryland leg and thigh still connected in a single piece; bones and skin intact.
tenderloin thin strip of meat lying just under the breast.

thigh cutlet thigh with skin and centre bone intact; sometimes found skinned with bone intact.
thigh fillet thigh with skin and centre bone removed.

CHICKPEAS also called garbanzos, hummus or channa; a sandy-coloured, irregularly round legume with a firm texture (even after cooking), a floury mouth-feel and a robust nutty flavour. Available canned or dried (the latter need several hours reconstituting in cold water before being used).

CHILLI available in many different types and sizes. Use rubber gloves when seeding and chopping fresh chillies as they can burn your skin. Removing seeds and membranes lessens the heat level.
cayenne pepper a long, thin-fleshed, extremely hot red chilli usually sold dried and ground.
flakes dried, deep-red, dehydrated chilli slices and whole seeds; good for use in cooking or as a condiment for sprinkling over cooked foods.
powder the Asian variety, made from dried ground thai chillies, is the hottest; it can be used as a substitute for fresh chillies in the proportion of ½ teaspoon ground chilli powder to 1 medium chopped fresh chilli.
red thai also known as "scuds"; tiny, very hot and bright red in colour.

CHIVES related to the onion and leek; has a subtle onion flavour. Used more for flavour than as an ingredient; chopped finely, they're good in sauces, dressings or as a garnish.

CINNAMON available as sticks (or quills) or ground; is the dried inner bark of the shoots of the cinnamon tree.

CLOVES dried flower buds of a tropical tree; can be used whole or in ground form. They have a strong scent and taste so should be used sparingly.

CORIANDER also known as cilantro, pak chee or chinese parsley; bright-green-leafed herb having both pungent aroma and taste. *Coriander seeds* are dried and sold either whole or ground, and neither form tastes like the fresh leaf, but rather like an acrid combination of sage and caraway.

GLOSSARY

COUSCOUS a fine, grain-like cereal product made from semolina. A semolina flour and water dough is sieved then dehydrated to produce minuscule, even-sized pellets of couscous; it is rehydrated by steaming or with the addition of a warm liquid and swells to three or four times its original size; eaten like rice with a tagine, as a side dish or salad ingredient.

CREAM we used fresh cream, unless otherwise stated. Also known as pure cream and pouring cream.

CUMIN also known as zeera or comino; is the dried seed of a plant related to the parsley family. It has a spicy, almost curry-like flavour. Also available ground. *Black cumin seeds* are smaller than standard cumin, and dark brown rather than true black; they are often mistakenly confused with kalonji (nigella) seeds.

CURRANTS, DRIED tiny, almost black, raisins from a grape native to Corinth, Greece. These are not the same as fresh currants, which are the fruit of a plant in the gooseberry family.

DATE fruit of the date palm tree, eaten fresh or dried, on their own or in prepared dishes. About 4cm to 6cm in length, oval and plump, thin-skinned, with a honey-sweet flavour and sticky texture.

DILL also known as dill weed; used fresh or dried, in seed form or ground; has a sweet anise/celery flavour with distinctive feathery, frond-like fresh leaves.

EGGPLANT also known as aubergine; ranges in size from tiny to very large and in colour from pale green to deep purple. Can be purchased char-grilled, packed in oil, in jars. *Baby eggplant* is also available and is also known as finger or japanese eggplant.

FENNEL also known as finocchio or anise; a crunchy green vegetable slightly resembling celery; also sometimes the name given to the dried seeds of the plant, which have a stronger licorice flavour.

FETTA a crumbly goat- or sheep-milk cheese with a sharp salty taste.

FIGS vary in skin and flesh colour according to type, not ripeness; when ripe, figs should be unblemished and bursting with flavour; nectar beads at the base indicate when a fig is at its best. Figs may also be glacéd (candied), dried or canned in sugar syrup.

FISH SAUCE also called nam pla or nuoc nam; made from pulverised salted fermented fish, most often anchovies. Has a pungent smell and strong taste, so use sparingly.

FLOUR, PLAIN an all-purpose flour made from wheat.

FRENCH-TRIMMED also sometimes just seen as "frenched"; a butchers' term referring to a cutting method where all excess sinew, gristle and fat from the bone end of meat cutlets, racks or shanks are removed and the bones scraped clean.

GINGER also known as green or root ginger; the thick gnarled root of a tropical plant. Can be kept, peeled, covered with dry sherry in a jar and refrigerated, or frozen in an airtight container. *Ground ginger*, also known as powdered ginger, is used as a flavouring in cakes, pies and puddings, but cannot be substituted for fresh (root) ginger.

HARISSA a North African paste made from dried red chillies, garlic, olive oil and caraway seeds; can be used as a rub for meat, an ingredient in sauces and dressings, or eaten on its own as a condiment. It is available, ready-made, from Middle-Eastern food shops and some supermarkets.

KALONJI SEEDS also known as nigella; are black, teardrop-shaped seeds used to impart a sharp, almost nutty flavour.

KITCHEN STRING made from a natural product such as cotton or hemp that will neither melt nor affect the flavour of the food during cooking as would a string made from synthetic materials.

KUMARA Polynesian name of orange-fleshed sweet potato often confused with yam.

LAMB
backstrap the larger fillet from a row of loin chops or cutlets.
shanks, french-trimmed also known as drumsticks or frenched shanks; end of the bone is discarded and the meat is trimmed.
sirloin a cut derived from a row of loin chops. Once the bone and fat are removed, the larger portion is referred to as the eye of the loin.

LAMINGTON PAN 20cm x 30cm slab cake pan, 3cm deep.

LENTILS (red, brown, yellow) dried pulses often identified by and named after their colour. *French green lentils* are green-blue, tiny lentils with a nutty, earthy flavour and a hardy nature that allows them to be rapidly cooked without disintegrating. They are a local cousin to the famous (and expensive) French lentils du puy.

MARJORAM an aromatic herb that is a member of the mint family; has long, thin, oval-shaped, pale-green leaves and a sweet taste similar to oregano. Used fresh or dried.

MINCE also known as ground meat, as in beef, veal, pork, lamb and chicken.

MUSTARD, DIJON also known as french mustard. A pale brown, creamy, distinctively flavoured, fairly mild french mustard.

MUSTARD SEEDS
black also known as brown mustard seeds; more pungent than the white variety; used frequently in curries.
white also known as yellow mustard seeds; used ground for mustard powder and in most prepared mustards.

NECTARINES smooth-skinned, slightly smaller cousin to the peach; juicy, with a rich and rather spicy flavour.

NUTMEG the dried nut of an evergreen tree native to Indonesia; usually found ground, but the flavour is more intense from a whole nut, available from spice shops, so it's best to grate your own with a fine grater.

OIL
cooking-oil spray we use a cholesterol-free cooking spray made from canola oil.
olive made from ripened olives. *Extra virgin* and *virgin* are the first and second press of the olives and are therefore considered the best; the *extra light* or *light* name on other types refers to taste not fat levels.
vegetable any of a number of oils sourced from plant rather than animal fats.

OKRA also known as bamia or lady fingers. A green, ridged, oblong pod with a furry skin. Native to Africa, this vegetable is used in Indian, Middle Eastern and South American cooking; it can be eaten on its own, in casseroles, or can be used to thicken stews.

OLIVES, NIÇOISE small black olives.

ONION
baby also known as cocktail or pickling onions.
brown and white are interchangeable. Their pungent flesh adds flavour to many dishes.
green also known as scallion or, incorrectly, shallot; an immature onion picked before the bulb has formed, having a long, bright-green edible stalk.
red also known as spanish, red spanish or bermuda onion; a sweet-flavoured, large, purple-red onion.
shallots also called french shallots, golden shallots or eschalots. Small, elongated, brown-skinned members of the onion family.

ORANGE FLOWER WATER concentrated flavouring made from orange blossoms. Available from Middle-Eastern food stores and some supermarkets and delicatessens. Cannot be substituted with citrus flavourings, as the taste is completely different.

OREGANO also known as wild marjoram; has a woody stalk with clumps of tiny, dark green leaves that have a pungent, peppery flavour and are used fresh or dried.

PAPRIKA ground dried sweet red capsicum (bell pepper); there are many types available, including sweet, hot, mild and smoked.

PARSLEY, FLAT-LEAF also known as italian or continental parsley.

PASTRY, FILLO also known as phyllo; tissue-thin pastry sheets purchased chilled or frozen.

PASTRY, READY-ROLLED SHORTCRUST packaged sheets of frozen shortcrust pastry available from supermarkets.

PATTY-PAN SQUASH also known as crookneck or custard marrow pumpkins; a round, slightly flat summer squash being yellow to pale-green in colour and having a scalloped edge. Harvested young, it has a firm white flesh and a distinct flavour.

PEPITAS pale green kernels of dried pumpkin seeds; they can be bought plain or salted.

PINE NUTS also known as pignoli; not, in fact, a nut, but a small, cream-coloured kernel from pine cones. They are best roasted before use to bring out the flavour.

PISTACHIOS green, delicately flavoured nuts inside hard off-white shells. Available salted or unsalted, shelled or unshelled.

PLUM SAUCE a thick, sweet and sour dipping sauce made from plums, vinegar, sugar, chillies and spices.

PRESERVED LEMON a North African specialty, the citrus is preserved, usually whole, in a mixture of salt and lemon juice or oil. To use, remove and discard pulp, squeeze juice from rind, then rinse rind well before slicing thinly. Available from specialty food shops and delicatessens.

PRUNES commercially or sun-dried plums; store in the fridge.

QUINCE yellow-skinned fruit with hard texture and an astringent, tart taste; eaten cooked or as a preserve. Long, slow cooking makes the flesh a deep rose pink.

RICE
basmati a white, fragrant long-grained rice; the grains fluff up when cooked. It should be washed several times before cooking.
calrose a medium grain, extremely versatile, rice; can substituted for short- or long-grain rices if necessary.
white long-grain white, elongated grains that remain separate when cooked; an extremely popular steaming rice.

SAFFRON stigma of a member of the crocus family, available ground or in strands; imparts a yellow-orange colour to food once infused. The quality can vary greatly; the best is the most expensive spice in the world.

SEMOLINA made from durum wheat milled into various textured granules, all of these finer than flour.

SESAME SEEDS black and white are the most common of these tiny oval seeds.

SHALLOT see onion.

SPINACH also known as english spinach and, incorrectly, silver beet.

SPLIT PEAS also known as field peas; green or yellow pulse grown especially for drying, split in half along a centre seam.

STAR ANISE a dried star-shaped pod whose seeds have an astringent aniseed flavour.

STOCK 1 cup (250ml) stock is the equivalent of 1 cup (250ml) water plus 1 crumbled stock cube (or 1 teaspoon stock powder).

SUGAR
brown an extremely soft, finely granulated sugar retaining molasses for its characteristic colour and flavour.
caster also known as superfine or finely granulated table sugar.
white coarse, granulated table sugar, also known as crystal sugar.

SULTANAS dried grapes; also known as golden raisins.

SUMAC a purple-red, astringent spice ground from berries growing on shrubs that flourish wild around the Mediterranean; adds a tart, lemony flavour to dips and dressings. Available from Middle-Eastern food stores and major supermarkets.

TAHINI sesame seed paste available from Middle-Eastern food stores, health food stores and major supermarkets.

TAMARIND the tamarind tree produces clusters of hairy brown pods, each of which is filled with seeds and a viscous pulp that are dried and pressed into the blocks of tamarind found in Asian food shops. Gives a sweet-sour, slightly astringent taste to marinades, pastes, sauces and dressings.

TAMARIND CONCENTRATE (or paste) the commercial result of the distillation of tamarind juice into a condensed, compacted paste.

THYME a member of the mint family; has tiny grey-green leaves that give off a pungent minty, light-lemon aroma. Dried thyme comes in both leaf and powdered form.

TOMATOES
canned whole peeled tomatoes in natural juices; available crushed, chopped or diced, sometimes unsalted or reduced salt.
cherry also known as tiny tim or tom thumb tomatoes; small and round.
egg also called plum or roma, these are smallish, oval-shaped tomatoes.
grape small, long oval-shaped tomatoes with a good tomato flavour.
puree canned pureed tomatoes (not tomato paste); substitute with fresh peeled and pureed tomatoes.
sun-dried tomato pieces that have been dried with salt; this dehydrates the tomato and concentrates the flavour. We use sun-dried tomatoes packaged in oil, unless otherwise specified.
truss small vine-ripened tomatoes with vine still attached.

TURMERIC also known as kamin; is a rhizome related to galangal and ginger. Must be grated or pounded to release its somewhat acrid aroma and pungent flavour. Known for the golden colour it imparts. Fresh turmeric can be substituted with the more common dried powder (use 2 teaspoons of ground turmeric plus a teaspoon of sugar for every 20g of fresh turmeric called for in a recipe).

VANILLA
bean dried, long, thin pod from a tropical golden orchid grown in Central and South America and Tahiti; the minuscule black seeds inside the bean are used to impart a luscious vanilla flavour in baking and desserts.
extract obtained from vanilla beans infused in water; a non-alcoholic version of essence.

VINEGAR
balsamic originally from Modena, Italy, there are now many balsamic vinegars on the market ranging in pungency and quality depending on how, and for how long, they have been aged. Quality can be determined up to a point by price; use the most expensive sparingly.
cider made from fermented apples.
red wine made from red wine.
white wine made from white wine.

ZA'ATAR a blend of whole roasted sesame seeds, sumac and crushed dried herbs such as wild marjoram and thyme. Available in delicatessens and specialty food stores.

ZUCCHINI also known as courgette; small, pale- or dark-green, yellow or white vegetable belonging to the squash family. Harvested when young, its edible flowers can be stuffed then deep-fried or oven-baked to make a delicious appetizer.

MEASURES

One Australian metric measuring cup holds approximately 250ml; one Australian metric tablespoon holds 20ml; one Australian metric teaspoon holds 5ml.

The difference between one country's measuring cups and another's is within a two- or three-teaspoon variance, and will not affect your cooking results. North America, New Zealand and the United Kingdom use a 15ml tablespoon.

All cup and spoon measurements are level. The most accurate way of measuring dry ingredients is to weigh them. When measuring liquids, use a clear glass or plastic jug with the metric markings.

We use large eggs with an average weight of 60g.

DRY MEASURES

METRIC	IMPERIAL
15g	½oz
30g	1oz
60g	2oz
90g	3oz
125g	4oz (¼lb)
155g	5oz
185g	6oz
220g	7oz
250g	8oz (½lb)
280g	9oz
315g	10oz
345g	11oz
375g	12oz (¾lb)
410g	13oz
440g	14oz
470g	15oz
500g	16oz (1lb)
750g	24oz (1½lb)
1kg	32oz (2lb)

LIQUID MEASURES

METRIC	IMPERIAL
30ml	1 fluid oz
60ml	2 fluid oz
100ml	3 fluid oz
125ml	4 fluid oz
150ml	5 fluid oz (¼ pint/1 gill)
190ml	6 fluid oz
250ml	8 fluid oz
300ml	10 fluid oz (½ pint)
500ml	16 fluid oz
600ml	20 fluid oz (1 pint)
1000ml (1 litre)	1¾ pints

LENGTH MEASURES

METRIC	IMPERIAL
3mm	⅛in
6mm	¼in
1cm	½in
2cm	¾in
2.5cm	1in
5cm	2in
6cm	2½in
8cm	3in
10cm	4in
13cm	5in
15cm	6in
18cm	7in
20cm	8in
23cm	9in
25cm	10in
28cm	11in
30cm	12in (1ft)

OVEN TEMPERATURES

These oven temperatures are only a guide for conventional ovens.
For fan-forced ovens, check the manufacturer's manual.

	°C (CELSIUS)	°F (FAHRENHEIT)	GAS MARK
Very slow	120	250	½
Slow	150	275-300	1-2
Moderately slow	160	325	3
Moderate	180	350-375	4-5
Moderately hot	200	400	6
Hot	220	425-450	7-8
Very hot	240	475	9

CONVERSION CHART

INDEX

ARE YOU MISSING SOME OF THE WORLD'S FAVOURITE COOKBOOKS?

The Australian Women's Weekly Cookbooks are available from bookshops, cookshops, supermarkets and other stores all over the world. You can also buy direct from the publisher, using the order form below.

TITLE	RRP	QTY	TITLE	RRP	QTY
Asian, Meals in Minutes	£6.99		Japanese Cooking Class	£6.99	
Babies & Toddlers Good Food	£6.99		Just For One	£6.99	
Barbecue Meals In Minutes	£6.99		Kids' Birthday Cakes	£6.99	
Beginners Cooking Class	£6.99		Kids Cooking	£6.99	
Beginners Simple Meals	£6.99		Kids' Cooking Step-by-Step	£6.99	
Beginners Thai	£6.99		Lean Food	£6.99	
Best Food	£6.99		Low-carb, Low-fat	£6.99	
Best Food Desserts	£6.99		Low-fat Feasts	£6.99	
Best Food Fast	£6.99		Low-fat Food For Life	£6.99	
Best Food Mains	£6.99		Low-fat Meals in Minutes	£6.99	
Cafe Classics	£6.99		Main Course Salads	£6.99	
Cakes Biscuits & Slices	£6.99		Mexican	£6.99	
Cakes Cooking Class	£6.99		Middle Eastern Cooking Class	£6.99	
Caribbean Cooking	£6.99		Midweek Meals in Minutes	£6.99	
Casseroles	£6.99		Moroccan & the Foods of North Africa	£6.99	
Casseroles & Slow-Cooked Classics	£6.99		Muffins, Scones & Breads	£6.99	
Cheesecakes: baked and chilled	£6.99		New Casseroles	£6.99	
Chicken	£6.99		New Classics	£6.99	
Chicken Meals in Minutes	£6.99		New Curries	£6.99	
Chinese Cooking Class	£6.99		New Finger Food	£6.99	
Christmas Cooking	£6.99		New Salads	£6.99	
Chocolate	£6.99		Party Food and Drink	£6.99	
Cocktails	£6.99		Pasta Meals in Minutes	£6.99	
Cooking for Friends	£6.99		Potatoes	£6.99	
Cupcakes & Fairycakes	£6.99		Salads: Simple, Fast & Fresh	£6.99	
Detox	£6.99		Saucery	£6.99	
Dinner Beef	£6.99		Sauces Salsas & Dressings	£6.99	
Dinner Lamb	£6.99		Sensational Stir-Fries	£6.99	
Dinner Seafood	£6.99		Slim	£6.99	
Easy Curry	£6.99		Stir-fry	£6.99	
Easy Spanish-Style	£6.99		Superfoods for Exam Success	£6.99	
Essential Soup	£6.99		Sweet Old Fashioned Favourites	£6.99	
Foods that Fight Back	£6.99		Tapas Mezze Antipasto & other bites	£6.99	
French Food, New	£6.99		Thai Cooking Class	£6.99	
Fresh Food for Babies & Toddlers	£6.99		Traditional Italian	£6.99	
Good Food Fast	£6.99		Vegetarian Meals in Minutes	£6.99	
Great Lamb Cookbook	£6.99		Vegie Food	£6.99	
Greek Cooking Class	£6.99		Wicked Sweet Indulgences	£6.99	
Grills	£6.99		Wok, Meals in Minutes	£6.99	
Healthy Heart Cookbook	£6.99				
Indian Cooking Class	£6.99		TOTAL COST:	£	

Mr/Mrs/Ms _____

Address _____

_____ Postcode _____

Day time phone _____ Email* (optional) _____

I enclose my cheque/money order for £ _____

or please charge £ _____

to my: ☐ Access ☐ Mastercard ☐ Visa ☐ Diners Club

PLEASE NOTE: WE DO NOT ACCEPT SWITCH OR ELECTRON CARDS

Card number | | | | | | | | | | | | | | | | |

Expiry date _____ 3 digit security code *(found on reverse of card)* _____

Cardholder's name_____ Signature _____

To order: Mail or fax – photocopy or complete the order form above, and send your credit card details or cheque payable to: Australian Consolidated Press (UK), Moulton Park Business Centre, Red House Road, Moulton Park, Northampton NN3 6AQ, phone (+44) (0) 1604 497531 fax (+44) (0) 1604 497533, e-mail books@acpuk.com or order online at www.acpuk.com
Non-UK residents: We accept the credit cards listed on the coupon, or cheques, drafts or International Money Orders payable in sterling and drawn on a UK bank. Credit card charges are at the exchange rate current at the time of payment.
Postage and packing UK: Add £1.00 per order plus 50p per book.
Postage and packing overseas: Add £2.00 per order plus £1.00 per book.
All pricing current at time of going to press and subject to change/availability.
Offer ends 31.12.2007

* By including your email address, you consent to receipt of any email regarding this magazine, and other emails which inform you of ACP's other publications, products, services and events, and to promote third party goods and services you may be interested in.